PRAISE FOR TEXAS PATRIARCH

"The story that Doug has put together is one that captures the raw emotion of a family fractured in the loss of their patriarch and the turbulent journey they have weathered to rebuild."

—Roger Staubach, former Dallas Cowboys quarterback, executive chairman of Jones Lang LaSalle

"There is nobody more prepared to write about the saga of a great Texas family than Doug Box. His legendary father, Cloyce, is like someone out of central casting. And what happened to Doug and his three brothers is something out of a best-selling novel. Get ready to shake your head in pure amazement."

—Skip Hollandsworth, executive editor of *Texas Monthly* magazine

"Poignant lessons for families in business together. Doug Box's chronicle of the turmoil his own family endured serves as an insightful example of what not to do when in business with your family."

—Thomas O. Hicks, chairman of Hicks Holdings, former owner of the Texas Rangers and the Dallas Stars

"A powerful lesson for anyone considering going into business with their family. Readers can learn from the mistakes Doug Box and his family made that nearly cost them both their family business and their family dynamic."

—Harlan Crow, real estate developer and philanthropist

"If Edna Ferber were still alive and writing she could have based her plot of *Giant* on the conflicts of the warring sons of the legendary rancher, oilman, and football hero Cloyce Box. This is a outsized story of North Texas and even more spectacular than fiction. So which of the brothers is most like Jett Rink? I visited the mansion several times before the fire when it was at its grandest during the Cattle Baron's Ball and 1984 Republican Convention, so I have great memories of the original Southfork Ranch . . . The TV show "Dallas" would have been more realistic if that ranch had been used for the whole series . . . it was the ultimate symbol of Dallas power and wealth."

—Nancy Smith, former society editor of the *Dallas Morning News*

"Our ranches were fairly close to each other and I grew up admiring this family and their beautiful estate in Frisco, Texas. It's a shame they went through such hard times—relationally and financially. Doug's experiences and work putting this book together... should be a helpful knowledge bank for all of us to use as our families grow more diverse across generations with shared asset ownership. From all of us families that are still trying to stay together in some way, thank you Doug. I know this wasn't easy to write, but hopefully your experiences will help many from going down the same path."

—Clint Haggard, founder and CEO of Clint Haggard
Family Advisors, fifth-generation Texan

"Texas Patriarch is the unvarnished story of an iconic Texas family as they travel from rags to riches to conflict. Written with stinging imagery and an unflinching style, Doug movingly describes the love, the pitfalls and inherent conflicts within all families struggling with legacies, dysfunction, and wealth. A quintessential Texas story."

—Wallace L. Hall Jr, founder of Wetland Partners and member of
the University of Texas System Board of Regents

"This is a story about Texas. A larger-than-life personality who built a business, but made sacrifices along the way. It tells a real-life story of how success can corrupt and how families are often left to pick up the pieces. There is something in it for everyone."

—Kenneth Hersh, cofounder and chairman of
NGP Energy Capital Management

"Most family stories are about heroic success and wonderful achievements. Rarely do we have the opportunity to get behind the scenes and hear the real or the whole story. This account, by a caring son, is about how personal demons from one's past and inner vulnerabilities can derail the most impressive success. The rise and fall of a family is a theme of books and movies, but we rarely get a personal and honest account of how that takes place. Doug tells an unsparing tale about his family, a larger-than-life father, and how his generation struggled to come to terms with his legacy. What is most amazing about this story is Doug's ability to tell the story straight and honestly, without a great deal of personal commentary. It is at times chilling but the story is a cautionary tale that is relevant to any family business moving across generations."

—Dennis Jaffe, professor emeritus at Saybrook University, family business consultant and educator for more than 40 years

"*Texas Patriarch* is a must-read for all family members who have a legacy to protect. Sharing his unique perspective on what many successful families have grappled with, Doug mesmerizes us with the untold story of the rise and fall of the one of the most successful American families. With candor and courage, he describes the devastating conflict that all but destroyed his family while giving us hope that family bonds ultimately can transcend the thirst for money and power."

—Blair Trippe, coauthor of *Deconstructing Conflict: Understanding Family Business, Shared Wealth and Power*

"*Texas Patriarch*, Doug Box's book about his father is a compelling read and a tour de force on the toxic impact a driven entrepreneur can have on his family. As a result of his own childhood, Cloyce Box was a deeply wounded, scarred man. He passed those scars and wounds on to his sons and others in his life through all his dealings. Doug's keen insights are testimony to the personal work he has done to understand his family. It is also evidence of how difficult it is to function independently and effectively when the entire family system is enmeshed and dysfunctional. I applaud Doug for his honesty and candor in telling the story. *Texas Patriarch* is an excellent text for those who wish to study entrepreneurs, their families, and the complexity of decision–making in such family systems. This is an important book for any family business library."

—David Bork, CEO of Family Business Matters, author of *The Little Red Book of Family Business*

TEXAS
PATRIARCH

Douglas D B

TEXAS PATRIARCH
A Legacy Lost

DOUGLAS D BOX

GREENLEAF
BOOK GROUP PRESS

In some instances, the names and identifying characteristics of persons referenced in this book have been changed to protect their privacy.

Published by Greenleaf Book Group Press
Austin, Texas
www.gbgpress.com

Distributed by Greenleaf Book Group

For ordering information or special discounts for bulk purchases, please contact Greenleaf Book Group at PO Box 91869, Austin, TX 78709, 512.891.6100.

Design and composition by Greenleaf Book Group
Cover design by Greenleaf Book Group

Cataloging-in-Publication data is available.

Print ISBN: 978-1-62634-297-2

eBook ISBN: 978-1-62634-298-9

Part of the Tree Neutral® program, which offsets the number of trees consumed in the production and printing of this book by taking proactive steps, such as planting trees in direct proportion to the number of trees used: www.treeneutral.com

TreeNeutral

Printed in the United States of America on acid-free paper

16 17 18 19 20 21   10 9 8 7 6 5 4 3 2 1

First Edition

To my mother, Fern Box, who loved and
supported all of us unconditionally, and to my father,
Cloyce Box, who was the champion of our world.

"All men dream, but not equally. Those who dream by night in the dusty recesses of their minds, wake in the day to find that it was vanity. But the dreamers of the day are dangerous men, for they may act on their dreams with open eyes, to make them possible."

—T. E. LAWRENCE

CONTENTS

PREFACE

My family came to Texas because of war. In 1836 my great-great-grandfather was only twenty-two years old when he and three of his cousins rode down from Tennessee to Houston to fight in the decisive battle of the Texas Revolution—the Battle of San Jacinto.

James Edward Box, John Andrews Box, Nelson Box, and Thomas Griffin Box fought with the 1st Company, 2nd Regiment of the Texas Volunteers at San Jacinto. All of them survived the fighting that day, and each of their names is inscribed on the San Jacinto monument located near the Houston Ship Channel.

My great-grandfather, Robert Douthit Box Sr., rode with the Confederate Cavalry during the Civil War. He was captured near Arkansas Point by Union forces and later released. My grandfather, Robert Douthit Box Jr., was drafted into the army and fought in France during World War I. My father Cloyce and his twin brother, Boyce Box, both served in World War II as well as the Korean conflict as officers in the US Marines Corps Reserves.

Unlike the generations before me, the closest I ever came to military service was watching the Vietnam War on the *CBS Evening News* with Walter Cronkite. As I grew older, however, I found myself drafted into a very different kind of struggle.

Historians are quick to point out that the costliest of all human conflict is a civil war because there can be no winners—only losers. A family business war is a lot like that. It's a form of corporate suicide in which family members often destroy the business as well as important relationships. What took place between my three older brothers and me as we tried to manage the business empire our father left to us is a saga as big as our home state.

My story begins with a true Texas legend: Cloyce Kennedy Box, a man who worked his way off a dirt-poor farm onto the pro football field and into the boardroom of a Fortune 500 company. In addition to being an athlete and corporate superstar, he was also my father.

Dad was larger than life, his rise marked with achievement and acclaim. Abandoned by his own father at the age of twelve, he suffered incredible hardship growing up on a Depression-era farm in central Texas. His ticket out of poverty was his talent on the gridiron. Later, he built a business empire with the same hard work, discipline, and focus he'd demonstrated on the playing field. My father's business world thrived, but his death sparked conflicts between family members that eventually destroyed the wealth he had worked so hard to accumulate.

Families with substantial financial resources often face unique challenges. For more than a decade, I've worked as an advisor to family-based enterprises, many of whom struggle with the same issues associated with wealth that my family encountered.

As you read through our story, compare it to your own. My hope is that it will give you a better chance of maintaining one of the most valuable things in life—healthy family relationships—while achieving financial and business success.

PROLOGUE

Flying a plane isn't as hard as it's cracked up to be. It's actually quite easy once you've reached cruising altitude. Takeoff and landing are the real tests of a pilot—the hair-trigger balancing act of monitoring gauges and flipping levers—but staying aloft is a simple matter of sitting back and allowing the bird to fly. I wasn't aware of this the first time my father switched over the controls of his Beechcraft Bonanza to me and said, "Here, Doug, fly.

"Watch out for planes," he added as he reclined his seat.

Watch out for planes? I thought. *That's it? That's all the instruction I'm going to get?* I was fifteen, barely old enough to drive a car, much less fly a plane.

Dad planned to nap during the two-hour flight to New Mexico. It was a trip he made frequently, often with me or one of my three brothers in the cockpit, to see his quarter horses run at Ruidoso Downs. Horse racing is the sport of kings, and that plane allowed him to travel from Dallas, Texas, to kingdoms near and far in order to keep up appearances and expand his growing oil empire.

I, on the other hand, was white-knuckled at the controls, praying I could live up to my father's expectations and keep us above the ridgebacks of the Sierra Blanca mountain range a mere 13,500 feet below.

The truth is, I hated flying with my father. Most people equate private planes with luxury, but to me, flying was a test of how much fear I was willing to swallow without letting on that if it were up to me, I'd bike the entire way to New Mexico. Hell, I'd even crawl.

Adding to my sense of unease was something my pilot cousin, Jimmy Bradford, had recently confessed to me. "Your dad's flying really bothers me."

"Why's that?" I'd asked.

"He doesn't follow the rules worth a darn," Jimmy had said. "He cuts a lot of corners."

Cloyce Box wasn't the kind of man who needed introductions. Even for those who knew nothing of his career catching touchdown passes for the Detroit Lions, or his rise to corporate fame with George A. Fuller Construction, or even his sprawling Texas ranch featured in the *Dallas* TV series, his tall, straight stature, striking blue eyes, and confident poise broadcast that he was a man of influence.

A poor farm boy from rural Texas who scaled the American dream, my father was admired and adored by just about everyone who knew him. From a young age, I knew of his rags-to-riches struggle growing up dirt poor. His ambition had no bounds, no limitations. But the legendary man was not the same one I knew as my father when I was growing up. That person was far more elusive.

Throughout the two-hour flight, one of the rare times I was alone with my father, we would hardly exchange more than a few words above the roar of the twin-engine aircraft. Nor do I think, given the opportunity, that I could have relaxed enough to open up to my father, a man who applied his Marine Corps training to childrearing. Nevertheless, I couldn't help but wonder: *Who was this man?*

And consequently: *Who was I?*

My father's influence on my brothers and me only grew stronger with time. Being the son of a Texas patriarch came with privilege and excitement, but it also came with a price: a harness that kept us closely linked to our larger-than-life father, for better or worse. I never felt the weight of that connection more than when I was in the cockpit high above the mountains, navigating through the clear blue sky with nothing but my dumb luck and his merciful assistance to keep us from crashing.

High up in the air, earthly problems grow small and the truly important things gain clarity. Pilots describe feelings of peace and introspection from such a vantage point. For me, there was no such revelation. Here I was with the man who seemed in control of my fate—both figuratively and literally—but I gained no further insight into the dangers that lay ahead. I wasn't sure what Jimmy meant about my father's flying, but I had a funny feeling I was about to find out.

After two hours had passed and the plane was still in the air, I eased up on the control yoke and enjoyed the view of the snaking rivers and textured earth below. I thought about the rest of the day—a hurried drive to the track, a few hellos and quick good-byes. Dad loved to fly, but no sooner did he set foot out of his plane than he was itching to get back in. He maintained a strict time limit on how long he could be away from Dallas, away from work. It was a short but invisible self-imposed leash—the only one that seemed to exist in his life.

Something alerted him that it was time to make our final descent. He sat up and switched the gear back to his side so effortlessly that I had to wonder if he had been awake the entire time, if he had somehow heard my thoughts through the loud hum of the cockpit.

Dad prepared for landing, a process he had carried out time and again with rote precision. I sat back in my seat, relieved. I hadn't crashed the plane, but was in no way eager to be in it any longer than necessary. The thought of landing made me happy enough to kiss the ground.

My anxiety came roaring back when I realized that something was wrong. Very wrong.

"Sonofabitch!" Dad grumbled under his breath. His hand was at the dash, aggressively pressing down on a red lever to no avail. "Damn landing gear!" he said.

When you're up in a plane, even the smallest screw in the panel seems integral to keeping it afloat. My heart raced as I envisioned the nose plummeting toward the ground, all of the blurred greens and browns rushing into terrifying clarity. I was only fifteen, and I was about to die.

"Hold my sunglasses, goddammit." He picked up the radio and called down to the control tower. The speech was garbled over the roaring cockpit noise, but he must have received the information he needed. He pushed the gear aside and located a lever between the seats. Using the full force of his six-foot-four, 220-pound frame, he was able to crank the handle and manually deploy the landing gear. The ordeal must have lasted no more than two minutes, but it was as if I lived three lifetimes. I don't think Dad even broke a sweat.

The plane landed without any further complications.

I would fly many more trips with my father. Each flight produced a familiar lurch in my stomach.

*T*hroughout the years, people have asked me what it was like grow-ing up with such an extraordinary man for a father. What was Cloyce Box really like? And this is the image I always return to: flying thou-sands of feet in the air with no one but him at the controls, no one but my father to bail me out.

Growing up with a man like Cloyce Box, who came as close to Superman as any person who walked the earth, was fast-paced, high-flying, exhilarating, and sometimes terrifying. Dad was a success up to the very end. After all these years, I find myself wondering what it all meant to him— the wealth, the land, the grandeur. Would he have built his empire with the same vigor and unrelenting drive if he'd known that it would someday tear his family apart?

PART I

The Rise of a Texas Patriarch

"Make no little plans,
They have no magic to stir men's blood . . .
Make big plans; aim high in hope and work."

—Daniel Burnham

Chapter 1

CAMELOT

I can't help but hold on to the belief that my family was for the most part happy when I was a small boy. Perhaps I perceive my early years in the idyllic light of nostalgia. From infancy to the age of eight, I was blissfully naïve about the harsher realities of life. My brothers and I reaped the material benefits of our father's long hours at the office, and while we didn't see him much at home, Mother was there to offer nurturing and comfort.

Our family life in the late fifties and early sixties was the epitome of a popular television show: *Father Knows Best*. We all bought into that unspoken credo: my father, the breadwinner and provider of all things material, did indeed know best.

Our home was a modest ranch house on Park Lane near Midway Road in Dallas. There was nothing remarkable about it, nothing to make its white-painted brick veneer and low-hanging roofline stand out from the others on the block. The only special feature was the backyard, which was big enough to accommodate a full-sized basketball court. Dad had the concrete slab poured right after we moved in. My three brothers and I spent most of our time there, maniacally chasing each other around on bicycles, skateboards, and all kinds of scooters. If it had wheels on it, we probably had one.

A wooden tree house was perched in one corner of the backyard not far from the basketball court. Dad had a contractor come out and build it, so it was well made. It had a wooden stepladder that led up through a trap door. The tree house was painted white, the same color as our house. Dad liked to paint everything white. When someone once asked him why, he said: "Because then I'll know whether or not it's clean."

Our house was constantly inundated with neighborhood friends who lived right across the street. If the weather was nice, we'd all walk to school together at Walnut Hill Elementary, where I attended the first and second grades.

We also had a trampoline, a bit of a novelty at the time. So was child safety: the trampoline had no protective netting, nothing to prevent an errant kid from jumping too close to the tightly coiled springs and bouncing himself straight into the emergency room. But no one ever did. It didn't seem possible, not even when my second-oldest brother Gary convinced us to move the trampoline right up next to the treehouse so we could jump down onto the mat below.

Mom cooked most of our meals at home during the Park Lane era. We rarely went out to eat. Every evening, regardless of whether or not Dad was at home, the rest of us ate dinner as a family. Christine, the maid who helped my mother, left just before we sat down at the small table in the kitchen that served as our main dining area. The table was barely big enough for all of us to get around, yet the slightly cramped conditions only added to the close-knit magic of life on Park Lane. I can still remember the sight of us sitting at that little kitchen table with both of our parents there. Nothing ever made me happier than for all of us to be together.

Even when Dad was gone, his presence was still felt around the house. My oldest brother, Don, happily stepped into our father's shoes any chance he could. Seven years older than me, Don was the smartest and most articulate of all of us boys. He made straight As and even looked smart in thick, black-rimmed glasses that made him resemble a stoic Buddy Holly. When Don talked, I would sit there in awe of his worldly knowledge.

Tommy and Gary weren't as impressed with our long-winded brother. They were more the outdoorsy types. Gary and Tommy preferred doing things, like hunting or fishing, over talking about things.

A bit mischievous, Gary was also fascinated with fire. One day when he was nine years old, he said to me, "Hey, let's see if we can set the house on fire!"

"Okay!" At age five I was eager to please my older brothers.

Gary pulled out a box of wooden matches.

"If we burn down the house, will we get in trouble?" I was suddenly a little afraid.

"Naw," Gary assured me. "Besides, it'll be fun."

"Okay." I complied.

We built a tiny blaze right next to the house. I watched the small flames getting bigger. A moment or two later, I looked back up at him. "If we burn the house down, we won't have any place to sleep," I pointed out tentatively.

He gave me a disgusted look. "You're probably right." We stomped the blaze out with our shoes, and Gary skulked off, leaving me to be sure the smoking pyre didn't spark up again.

Tommy was the brother I was always the closest to, though as with any sibling relationship, there was always some friction between us.

I've sometimes wondered if I didn't get too used to being pushed around when I was growing up. There are times when I can remember being knocked around by the older boys, including my brothers and a few of my cousins. One day, when I was twelve, Tommy and I were sweeping out the big barn of our new house in Frisco, Texas. I smarted off to him, and he popped me in the mouth with the backside of a push broom. I don't think he meant to hit me quite as hard as he did, but the blow cut open both lips. Blood gushed from my mouth, and it hurt like hell. He didn't get in trouble for that. Mom and Dad didn't seem to punish him for the things he did to me as a kid. At least that's the way I remember it. Maybe I didn't complain loudly enough. I wanted the older kids to like me and didn't want them calling me a sissy.

But I was a bit of a smart aleck, and I did things to provoke my brothers as much as they did things back to me. For the most part, there were many more good times than bad, and all of us were close.

*T*he best times on Park Lane took place during the holidays.

One Christmas morning, long before daylight, my brothers and I woke in unison and dashed out of our barracks-style bedroom toward our silver aluminum Christmas tree. We couldn't wait a minute longer to see what Santa had brought us. Our parents, who must have been up all night, watched with excitement as we opened our presents. After we'd finished opening the airplanes, balls, soldiers, and toy guns, we learned there was another gift waiting for us. This one was not under the tree. It was tied to the cyclone fence just outside the sliding glass door to our backyard.

As dawn came over the fading darkness of that Christmas morning, it shed its light on a tall palomino. When we saw it, the four of us shrieked so loud that the horse tossed its head and shifted its weight back and forth on powerful legs. We almost broke through the glass window to get to the amazing creature.

Dad seemed more excited than we were. Anytime he was around

a horse, he wore an ear-to-ear grin. I don't believe any man ever loved horses more than my father did.

We all clambered outside. Tommy leaned forward and hugged the horse around its legs.

"Careful, Tommy, you might spook him," Dad warned, but Tommy wasn't the least bit scared of the horse.

"What's his name?" Gary asked.

"His name is Dan," Dad replied.

"Dan is my horse," Tom pronounced, "and I'm the only one who can ride him."

Determined to be the first one on the palomino, he reached up with both hands, signaling Dad to give him a boost. Dad let out a booming laugh at Tommy's enthusiasm. Once Tommy was atop the horse, Dad handed him the leather reins and tried to instruct him on how to ride. Tommy took off like a pro, riding bareback in his pajamas while the rest of us stood there in awe of how quickly he took to being in the saddle.

*B*ut one day, something happens that leaves me feeling like our home isn't always such a wonderful haven of boisterous fun.

I'm six years old, big enough to want my own box of crayons. At first, Mom won't get them for me. We have a whole drawerful at home, she says. But I'm tired of sharing crayons with my three older brothers. All the pointy little heads with their perfectly sharpened tips are gone once they have their way with them.

Mother finally gives in and buys me a brand new box of crayons. I especially like the fresh, waxy smell when I first open the box. I also like how the labels show the distinctive names of all the colors— Indian red, olive green, Prussian blue.

I live my life through the lens of an active imagination. In my mind, I'm a great artist. Therefore, a simple coloring book won't do. I need a canvas to draw on, a big one. The white walls of the bedroom I share with my brothers are perfect for what I want to do. I may not be old enough to go to school with Don, Gary, and Tommy, but by golly I'm old enough to draw on the walls.

I've been told more than a few times that drawing on the walls is off limits. My mother's even warned that she might spank me the next time it happens. "I'm gonna get the belt out," she likes to threaten. But her "belt" is a skinny decorative accessory from a cocktail dress, and even when she musters up the nerve to spank one of us boys, she can't make herself hit us hard enough to make it hurt. I'm not afraid of her or her belt.

I climb up onto the dresser and begin to draw. As I work, I hear a voice with a British accent speaking, as if to an audience gathered around to watch me. "Quiet, please. A great artist must have silence as he works." A quick glance over my shoulder reveals a room full of admirers, every eye filled with rapture.

Just as my creation is beginning to take shape, I'm disturbed by a different kind of sound. My father is home from work. Dad never comes home this early in the afternoon. But I recognize the unmistakable banging of the front door, the thud of heavy feet, and the scraping noise his briefcase makes when it slides across our brick entryway.

I scamper down from the dresser and stand near the doorway. Terror fills me as he enters my bedroom. My father is a giant of a man. He glances up at my scribbling on the wall, looks me in the eye, and says, "Did you draw on these walls?"

No words will come out of my mouth.

"I asked you a question," he growls. "Did you draw on these walls after you were told not to?"

I shake my head back and forth, denying the evidence behind me.

"Don't lie to me, son." Dad points a finger at the wall, his eyes fixed on me. His voice is louder now. "I want you to answer me. Did you draw on these walls?"

I can't get a single word out.

"That's it. I'm gonna give you a whipping."

Before he even touches me I throw myself facedown on my bed and begin to wail, "No, no, no, Daddy, please don't spank me!" I cup my hands around the sides of my head as if to protect myself from the worst.

I can't see a thing, but I feel plenty. First he uses his belt. His blows are like lightning bolts, swift and shocking.

"You're a bad, bad boy!" he yells over the noise of my wailing. "Don't you ever do that again!"

I bawl in a way I've never done before. Yet the spanking goes on. Now he is spanking my bottom with his open hand. Over and over he says, "You're a bad, bad boy" and, "Don't you ever do that again." Maybe this lasts only a few moments, but at age six my sense of time is so fluid it feels like forever. What if he's decided to kill me? Who could stop him?

Finally, he leaves the room. He makes no move to comfort me, even though I am still sobbing.

Not long after the spanking, my parents are getting dressed for a night on the town. Mom and Dad are putting the finishing touches on their evening wardrobe. I can always tell when they're going out by the familiar scent of aftershave and perfume. I don't want them to go out. It makes me anxious. I especially don't want my mother to leave.

I horse around outside their bedroom, trying to get their attention; maybe if I act cute and charming, I tell myself, they'll change their minds and stay home. But Dad yells at me to cut it out. His stern tone stirs memories of what happened the last time I disobeyed. And before I know it, a warm sensation flows down my pant leg.

Dad has literally scared the piss out of me.

/ never got over the spanking my father gave me that day, at least not during my childhood. It was the only time in my life he ever laid a hand on me. It was the only time he needed to.

Chapter 2

THE CHAPARRAL CLUB

One night in 1963, my mother announces that we are to get cleaned up and dressed in the clothes laid out on our beds. This has been happening more and more frequently as Dad has grown more and more successful. Our housekeeper, Christine, helps the four of us boys comb unruly hair and corral rogue loafers skulking under beds or in the back of our closets.

At age six, I dress quickly for these outings because I don't want to miss the exhilarating moment when my mother emerges from her bedroom. Once I pass inspection under Christine's critical eye, I linger in front of my parents' door, eager for a glimpse of my mother transformed.

Blonde with deep blue eyes, Fern Cunningham is a natural beauty, as pretty as any Hollywood movie star. It's easy to see how she caught Dad's eye when they met in a business law class at West Texas State Teachers College. When she flashed my father a bright smile, he noted her curves in all the right places, filling out the pretty blue print wrap dress that hugged her bosom and hips and brought out the color in her eyes. He appreciated her shapely calves and dainty feet in kitten heels.

Four children later, she still has her pinup figure. Adorned in a glamorous evening gown and jewelry, with her platinum hair piled high on her head in an upsweep, the sight of her dressed for a night on the town is as heady as the perfume she floats in. My mother is every bit a woman as Cloyce Box is a man.

On this particular night, we're going to the Chaparral Club. It's a dinner club that sits atop the Southland Life Building in downtown Dallas. It has great steaks and a live jazz band. My brothers and I love to peer down from the fiftieth-floor dining room at all of the neon lights strewn along the main streets of Dallas. The view inside is just as dazzling. The club is frequented by Dallas's big names, and it's always a thrill to spot the movers and shakers dining there. One night Tom Landry even came over to say hello.

We arrive before Dad, my brothers and I trailing along behind our mother like besotted fans. We aren't the only ones. Most heads turn when she walks by. But my demure mother is so devoted to my father that she never seems to notice the eye-popping stares.

The maître d' seats us at Dad's usual table in the center of the large dining room, strategically chosen so that he can hold court. While the four of us boys can cause quite a ruckus at times, we are well trained in social graces. Now, we nod and sit quietly while we wait for Dad to join us.

My oldest brother, Don, looks bored. At age thirteen, he is bookish and socially awkward. My next brother, Gary, has smuggled some small metal contraption made of gears into the restaurant. He is fiddling with it now in his lap, glancing furtively across the table at our mother every few minutes to make sure she hasn't caught him. Gary likes cars and machinery better than school. He likes to take things apart to see how they work and then tries to figure out how to put them back together again. Dad nicknamed him our "shade tree mechanic," which turns out to be an eerily correct prediction of who Gary turns out to be in his adult years.

Tommy, already good looking and charming at age eight, is the most like our father in temperament. He's the golden child whom everyone adores. He leans back in his chair grinning, soaking up the festive atmosphere of the room and pointing out all the people he recognizes from other evenings at the club as if he is a bona fide wheeler-dealer like Dad.

I am seated next to Mother. The place I most love to be is in her lap, but now that I am six my father frowns when he finds me there. She's babied me longer than my father would have preferred. It's true that I'm the baby of the family, and I'm a mama's boy. I'm also a bit insecure, as if I can sense some nebulous danger lurking around me. I've sucked my thumb for so long that my brothers tease me about it. But I am fearful at times and the habit soothes me. And I have this instinct—especially since the incident with the crayons the year before—that Mom is the only thing in the world I can truly count on.

Dad finally appears, stopping at table after table to shake hands with the other men dining there. He presses his lips to the powdered cheeks of the women as he makes his way through the crowded room, saying hello to the other businessmen who are eager to get in his good graces, knowing that they're all watching him with thinly veiled envy as he takes his seat next to the most glamorous woman in the room: his wife.

This night, Dad brings someone else along with him. This is not unusual. He loves a crowd, and he often invites colleagues from work to impress them with his picture-perfect family.

"Fern, boys, this is my new secretary, Jane Palmer," Dad announces as he shepherds a striking young brunette toward our table. "She's new to Dallas, so show her some genuine Texas hospitality." Daddy gestures to the waiter to bring another place setting. The waiter starts to make room for Jane next to shy Don, who looks panic-stricken at the thought of sitting beside the stylish, attractive twenty-one-year-old. Dad shoots the waiter a look before gesturing to his left, and the waiter hustles to cover his gaffe. Jane is to sit at Dad's side, so that my father is flanked by both beautiful women now seated at the table.

My impression of Jane Palmer is that she is a younger version of my mother. As the grownups make conversation, the two of them talk about how much they love music, and I learn that she plays the piano like Mom does, adding to my strange sense that she and my mother are somehow connected.

In spite of her sultry appearance, Jane seems to genuinely enjoy meeting all of us. She asks each of us boys about our favorite hobbies, and she tells us she enjoys bowling. Smitten by the alluring young woman, Tommy pipes up, "I can out-bowl anyone at this table." He challenges Jane to see who can bowl the most strikes, to which our father responds with a droll comment that Miss Palmer is too old for Tom to date.

That night was a good representation of the golden age of the Box family. My father had several careers in full swing, a beautiful wife, four healthy boys, and a house that was a mansion compared to the shack he'd grown up in.

I sometimes wonder what life would have been like if my father had found sufficient solace in a suburban home and family. But growing up dirt poor had left him with a driving need to ward off any possibility of future poverty. To do that, he had to amass a fortune.

As a result, my father became the quintessential workaholic who rarely took a day off—even on weekends. My parents even turned down an invitation to the JFK inauguration because Dad was too busy with work. As he grew more and more successful, this dedication let him provide for the family in bigger, more lavish ways. But since he was rarely at home, my brothers and I either enjoyed home life without him or visited him at his office. He was more intimate with his work colleagues than with his own children.

As a high-profile rising executive, Dad traveled a lot, and he spent so much time in New York that whenever our phone rang, Gary would blurt out, "He's gone to New York!" We often went to Manhattan as a family, too. I remember walking down Fifth Avenue with my father. He would stop, point up to some monstrous skyscraper, and say, "You see that building, Doug? I built that." I was so young that I took him literally. I tried to imagine him in work clothes and a hardhat, a pick and shovel in hand as he poured concrete or erected steel beams. I had trouble figuring out how he could do such things, but there was no doubt in my mind that he did. When Cloyce Box told you something, you believed him. You had to.

In New York, Dad spent time at places like the 21 Club and the Plaza Hotel, places he had only gawked at in wonder on his first visit to Manhattan, when he'd played basketball for West Texas State in the National Invitational Tournament at Madison Square Garden. Perhaps the opulence and wide variety of lifestyles he had seen on that trip to New York as a college kid were part of what made Dad so determined to succeed. And succeed he did. As a result of all of his hard work, my father had achieved the American dream. He had a lot to feel proud about.

But just as the last months of 1963 and the Kennedy assassination signaled the end of the American Camelot, it also marked the subtle beginning of our family's decline. Dad was an ambitious man, accustomed to using fierce determination to conquer a goal. Yet despite his accomplishments, he couldn't sit back and enjoy his success. No matter how much he accumulated, there was always some bigger dream to chase.

Dad wouldn't stop. He didn't have it in him to even slow down.

Chapter 3

JONESBORO

One Sunday morning, Dad hustles our mother and the four of us boys out of the house and into his '63 Cadillac de Ville sedan. My brothers push each other, jockeying for position in the window seats. At age seven, I know better than to join the fray. As the youngest, I'd get pummeled just for trying. I resign myself to being squashed in the middle between the others.

This is an unprecedented adventure. We go places with Dad all the time, but he likes to travel with an entourage of friends, schmoozing and conducting business along the way, so we share our charismatic father with a lot of people. I don't mind much. Most of the people are smart and interesting, like him. But this is our first time going somewhere without any of Dad's cronies. Something has compelled him to take us all to his hometown, some need to share with his sons a glimpse of the boy he was growing up, long before his hard-earned destiny of fame and fortune. To me, this lends the trip an air of reckless daring.

We barrel out of Dallas down I-35, the Cadillac's shark-like fins flaring out the back. The regal automobile commands awe, much as my father does. He entertains Mom with some story about the office.

My mother laughs prettily in response. We are together as a family with no one else along for the ride. That's all that matters.

Just past Waco, we exit the freeway and head west down toward Gatesville. After several hours passing through one-horse towns, we finally arrive, rather anticlimactically after all the suspense of the morning, in the forlorn little farm community of Jonesboro.

Dad pulls onto the side of the two-lane rural road. He turns around in the driver's seat and looks at us boys. Don has brought along a book and has his head stuck in it, as usual. But Gary, Tommy, and I are eager to see whatever Daddy wants to show us.

"You see that field right there?" He motions out the windshield. "That's where we used to pick cotton."

I look out at the dusty flats. All I see is a dilapidated wooden hut that looks like it will collapse the next time the wind blows. *It's nothing but a shack*, I think. *We drove all the way down here to look at* this?

Dad seems off in another world, seeing things before him that are invisible to the rest of us. "We used to plow those fields with horses. We didn't have no tractor. Ol' Blue and Ol' Silver." Suddenly he flings open his door and jumps out of the car.

"Cloyce, where are—" my mother begins.

Daddy interrupts her. "There's our old farmhouse. That's where we lived," he announces. "No electricity. No indoor plumbing. We got water from that ol' well."

It seems like he's talking to himself. "Rope cost a lot of money. Sometimes your Uncle Boyce and me'd get impatient and let that rope drop down the well. Momma'd be inside cookin', and she'd hear the squeaky noise of the pulley and know we'd let it go. Then she'd come runnin' out onto the front porch, slammin' the screen door behind her, and bawl us out. 'You're gonna wear that rope out,' she'd yell, 'and then I'm gonna wear *you* out!'"

A small grin plays over his mouth as Daddy mimics Grandma Zelma, but his eyes look sad. Our grandmother, ill most of her life with tuberculosis, lives near us in Dallas. I couldn't begin to find the lady my daddy is describing in the pale, fragile woman who rarely speaks and spooks me a little whenever she visits.

Dad continues describing the barren place before us. "You see that outhouse?" He smiles bashfully. "That's where we had to go. You had to use the Sears catalogue when you got done." He shakes his head. "Anyways, it all sure is different from what we have today, isn't it, boys?"

Mother speaks into the uneasy silence that falls upon us. "Your daddy's worked so hard and done so well," she says to us boys, although her words are meant for my father. "C'mon back in the car now and let's head on home, Cloyce. It'll be suppertime by the time we get back."

Mother's tone soothes me, if not my father. I haven't been moved to any kind of appreciation of the literally dirt-poor circumstances of Daddy's upbringing. I can't imagine the hardships he'd endured, although the vestiges of them are right in front of me. I just can't see my father, who drives a fancy car and flies all over the world on private jets, ever living in the rundown house that looks like little more than a pile of sticks.

Apparently, neither can my brothers. Don is pressed up against the window on his side of the car, reading away, willfully ignoring nine-year-old Tommy and eleven-year-old Gary, who are roughhousing again. I'm old enough to sense that this desolate landscape in front of us is important to my father, but I don't understand why. I don't really care. I'm just hoping we get back to Dallas before dark so we can shoot some hoops before bedtime.

I **had no way** of knowing at such a young age that our brief trip to Jonesboro would be my one and only chance to learn something from my father about who he'd been before he grew into a successful businessman. He never mentioned the farm again, not even when one of us boys reached some milestone like going off to college, which might have sparked heart-to-heart chats for other fathers and sons. Not for Cloyce Box. For a man with a flair for storytelling, he was reticent on the subject of his early years. We didn't ask, and Dad didn't tell. Perhaps he simply couldn't bear to relive it.

The Great Depression had stolen my father's childhood. My paternal grandfather, R. D. Box Jr., was only twenty-three years old when World War I broke out in Europe and his country called for his service. R. D. Jr. had a fragile disposition before he went off to war. He returned not hardened but rattled by his experiences in battle. A quiet man who kept to himself, he sought salvation in the land and set out to run his own farm.

Like many other poor, struggling families of the 1920s who relied on the land for their livelihoods, the Boxes of Jonesboro were rural, humble, and hardworking. Life on the farm wasn't easy. My grandparents and all four of their children—Janice, Cloyce, his twin Boyce, and Wilmuth (whom they called Tom after her father gave her the nickname) did backbreaking physical labor to survive. Yet I imagine that my father felt safe, secure, and well cared for during his early days. My grandmother was a woman of incredible strength and courage who raised my father and his siblings with an indomitable spirit and determination. R. D. Jr. wasn't much for interacting or playing with his kids, but he provided for them by toiling in the fields during the triple-digit heat of brutal Texas summers.

Everything changed on Tuesday, October 29, 1929. "Black Tuesday" kicked off a general economic decline, bringing about the Great

Depression. Few families were more vulnerable to such a cataclysm than the Boxes of Jonesboro. They were already dirt poor—how could they get any poorer?

The collapse in farm prices destroyed R. D. Jr.'s small-time operation. My grandfather felt a deep sense of shame and guilt as a result of his financial privation. R. D. Jr. had been drafted and forced to fight in a world war that cast a permanent shadow on the once carefree farm boy. The added strain of the Depression further weakened his belief in his ability to provide for his wife and children. He moved out of the farmhouse and in with his father, who lived nearby. Perhaps he found some respite there from the endless responsibilities of raising a family on a farm. But the relief wouldn't last.

On August 23, 1935, my great-grandfather, R. D. Box Sr., died. Now that he was gone, the responsibilities—the hungry children, the failing farm—all fell back on R. D. Jr. It was a fate he couldn't avoid. Like so many men of that era, he had to live with the shame of having no means to provide. It might have seemed to him that the world was coming to an end.

No one really knows what was going through his mind, but soon after R. D. Jr.'s father passed away, he made plans for his own departure. The decision may have come down to a choice between leaving and suicide.

He might have preferred to slip away without incident, but before he could take his leave, my twelve-year-old father confronted him.

"Daddy, what's going on?" Cloyce kicked nervously at the clods of dirt in front of the house. R. D. Jr. was placing a ratty bundle of clothing into the wagon. "Momma said something about you was leaving. You're not really leaving, are you?"

"I have to go, Cloyce. I can't stay here no more," R. D. Jr. replied.

Cloyce's mouth gaped open. "But Daddy, you can't just leave us here. You can't just run off and leave." His voice rose in despair. "We got nothing to eat! We're gonna die if you do!"

"You ain't gonna die, son." R. D. Jr. said, careful not to make eye contact. "Now go on and be a big man. This ain't none of yer business anyway."

There was a long pause. "For how long?" Cloyce finally asked.

R. D. Jr. said nothing.

"Dad!" Cloyce yelled sharply, as if his father had suddenly gone deaf. "When are you coming back?"

"I ain't coming back here no more, son."

R. D. Jr.'s face was set with grim determination. Perhaps he felt that the honest-to-God truth would be less painful than vague lies about returning soon.

"Tell me where you're going, Daddy," Cloyce pleaded. "Please tell me when you're coming back!"

"Never and a day," R. D. Jr. muttered under his breath.

"You can't just leave us here; we're gonna die if you do!" Cloyce's voice rose in despair.

"You ain't gonna die, son." R. D. Jr. brushed off his concerns. "Now go on and be a big man."

"We got nothing to eat!" Cloyce wailed, restraint stripped away by desperation.

R. D. Jr. shot back, "I told you I'm going away and I ain't never coming back. Now go on and git outta my way, boy." He threw his arm up as if shooing away a stray dog.

Cloyce doubled over, howling as if he'd just been shot. His twin brother, Boyce, who'd been watching the whole exchange from a distance, moved in closer.

"Come on now," he urged Cloyce, "just forget about him. He's gonna go, and there's nothing we can do about it."

"There sure as hell is!" Cloyce straightened up. "I'll kill the bastard!"

He lunged in the direction of his middle-aged father and beat at him with both fists. Boyce rushed up and bear-hugged his brother from behind. The boys typically got along well, as most twins do, but now Cloyce twisted around and turned his fury on Boyce.

"Sumbitch, let me go!" Cloyce yelled. "Git off me, godammit."

Boyce couldn't say a word, struggling as he was to restrain Cloyce.

"Git offa me!" Cloyce shouted again.

"You can't make him stay," Boyce managed to let out.

"Then I'll just have to kill him," Cloyce yelled.

"You ain't big enough to kill nobody," Boyce hollered back.

The two boys hit the ground, a gridlock of arms and legs rolling around in the dirt, kicking up dust, banging up against the wheel of R. D. Jr.'s wagon. Their dog Charlie mistook the whole thing as frolic and barked and snarled at them.

Zelma, Janice, and Tom rushed out onto the front porch. Thirteen-year-old Janice was so distraught that she didn't know who to be mad at the most. "Stop it right now, you two shit-asses!" she shouted in the direction of the wrestling match. Then, turning to her father, she bellowed: "You see what you've done here, Daddy? See what you've done to your family? Is this what you want?" Her voice caught in her throat.

Zelma put an arm around her eldest daughter's shoulders, her mouth set in a grim line of resignation. Little Tom, who was only eight, ran back into the house and hid under the bed to cry.

With madness rising all around him, R. D. Jr. jumped into the front seat of the wagon, snapped his reins, and yelled "Yah!" at the team of horses. The moving wagon ended the contest between Boyce and Cloyce. The two of them stood, locked arm in arm, watching in shock as their father rode off from the farm and out of their lives.

Chapter 4
THE TWIN TERRORS

Childhood ended for the Box kids on the day my grandfather left. His departure cast shame upon his wife and children. Divorce was so uncommon in those days that my grandmother was distraught and ostracized by the community. Yet even amid the whispers, Zelma held her head up high.

There's no such thing as part-time farming. Janice and the twins were old enough to pitch in with the chores after school and on weekends, but with R. D. Jr. gone and no adult male to work the farm, the family could no longer keep hogs. With no hogs or cash crop to sell, they had no income. Zelma kept chickens and turkeys and the vegetable garden, but she had no way to make any real money.

Cloyce and Boyce stepped into their father's shoes at age twelve and supported their mother and sisters. They took to selling cedar posts for cash. Thankfully there was lots of cedar around, but chopping it was hard work and could only be done in the winter. Summer was just too hot for the job. The twins cut big batches of the wood and tried to hide it for safekeeping, but someone once found their hidden stash and stole it all.

The boys looked for work wherever they could get it. My father spent the summer after eighth grade working on a farm miles away from the family homestead. He carried his small sack of belongings and kept it in the hay bale where he slept at night after toiling in the fields for the hottest months of the year. Finally, he met with the landowner to receive his payment: a burlap bag of onions, one of the few things Zelma was able to grow at home. The walk home that day was a long one, but it taught him a valuable lesson that he never forgot: before you make a deal, always know what you're getting.

*N*ot long after R. D. Jr.'s departure, Zelma was stricken with tuberculosis. There was little doubt that the damp, drafty farmhouse, a virtually uninhabitable dwelling, was the cause of her malady. Another factor had to be exhaustion. Zelma had practically worked herself to death.

County health officials feared an epidemic and sent my grandmother to a sanitarium for quarantine. In the midst of the Great Depression, the four Box kids suddenly had no one to care for them. Janice and Tom went to live with a foster family whom they affectionately called "Mom and Pop" Kitchens, while the school superintendent and head basketball coach, Mr. Pearly Thomas "P. T." Lemmons, took in Boyce and Cloyce. Mr. Lemmons became a surrogate father to the twins, paying for their school lunches and athletic shoes out of his own pocket.

For his entire life, education was important to Dad because it allowed him to escape the terrible circumstances of his upbringing. My father and his twin had never considered college a possibility. As far as they knew, higher education cost money, which they didn't have. It took a lot of convincing by Mr. Lemmons to make them understand that they could attend for free. All they had to do was play basketball. This would be their chance to get out of small-town Jonesboro and out of poverty. Their mother Zelma sent them down the road with her full blessing.

That summer, Cloyce and Boyce packed everything they owned in a single small bag and hitchhiked four hundred miles from Jonesboro to West Texas State Teachers College in Canyon, Texas. They were just a couple of wide-eyed country boys with two dollars between them, earned as payment for chopping cotton.

It took them several days to get to Canyon. They slept on the side of the road and ate sparingly to conserve their meager funds. A man picked them up in Plainview and let them out on the square in Canyon around midnight. Because of the late hour, they paid one of their two dollars for a hotel room. The next day, they spent the last of their money on food. When they walked over to the campus and checked into their dorm at five that afternoon, neither of them had a single cent in their pockets.

When the twins first arrived at the campus at West Texas State, they were intimidated. Canyon was just a small town, but the university campus with its three hundred sprawling acres of yellow brick buildings was the most impressive place the boys had ever been.

They were to meet with the athletic director, W. A. "Gus" Miller, who would have final approval over their scholarships. If they didn't get their scholarship, there was no way they could afford college, and they wanted to attend very badly. That's when Cloyce, particularly anxious about the interview, came up with an idea to make them appear more impressive to the athletic director—a story that became high drama as it was retold again and again at family gatherings.

"Hey Boyce," Dad whispered under his breath. "When we get in there, don't tell 'em we're from Jonesboro. Let's tell 'em we're from Waco."

"Why can't we tell 'em we're from Jonesboro?" Boyce asked.

"Shit, Boyce," Dad said, irritated. "If they find out we're from Jonesboro, they'll think we're a couple of country bumpkins that fell off a turd wagon. We'll never get our scholarship."

"I don't think we should lie," Boyce said.

"Just let me do the talking," Dad insisted.

Finally, Gus Miller invited the twins into his office and sat them down across from his desk. He couldn't help but be impressed by the size and maturity of the two farm boys. Though they had turned nineteen only a month before, they looked more like full-grown men.

"Hello there, Boyce," Gus Miller began after they shook hands. Looking over at my dad, he added, "and is it Clovis?"

"Cloyce," Dad replied. He was used to people mispronouncing his name.

"Got it!" Coach Miller grinned. "How 'bout that—Cloyce and Boyce! The Box twins!"

"Yessir," the twins agreed in unison, unsure how to respond to the coach's exuberance.

Coach Miller relaxed back into his chair. "Now tell me, boys, where'd y'all say you was from?"

"Uh, Waco, sir," Cloyce replied.

"Waco, really?"

Cloyce nodded vigorously. He shot a glance over at Boyce, who was biting his lower lip.

"Well, golly. The Box twins . . . Cloyce and Boyce." Coach Miller shifted around in his chair. He glanced down at some papers on his desk, and then he looked up again and leaned forward, as if he was about to share a secret.

"I gotta be honest with you boys." His voice dropped. His eyes darted back and forth between the twins. "There's another set of twins out there, but these boys is from Jonesboro. The stories we've heard about them two boys, you'd think they was somethin' the likes of the sons of Paul Bunyan. We just can't wait to meet 'em!"

Coach Miller waited a beat, then raised an eyebrow. "Y'all know anything 'bout them boys from Jonesboro?" he asked, feigning innocence.

Boyce glared at Cloyce. My father cleared his throat and said: "Well sir, we *are* from Jonesboro, sir. It's just that my brother Boyce here was too embarrassed to admit where we's from."

Chapter 5

VICTORY QUEEN

My mother was a small-town girl from rural Arkansas. Fern Cunningham had grown up poor like Dad. She didn't have big expectations in life. She'd been sheltered by her loving family, especially her father, Sam Cunningham, who'd doted on her. Despite her good looks and popularity, which won her the title of Victory Queen during her senior year of high school, she was a humble and down-to-earth woman.

The best time of her life was the four years she spent at West Texas State Teachers College. In her freshman year, she was crowned Sweetheart of the 350th College Training Detachment. She majored in business administration, joined a sorority, and played clarinet in the school band.

Like many women of her era, Fern was keen to find a husband. She'd wanted a man like her father—sweet, affectionate, and fun loving. Mother was well educated but not the least bit worldly. Cloyce Box was a complex, intriguing man, and my mother fell completely in love with his strength and capability.

For his part, Dad had been taken with Fern the first time they met. He had never seen anyone as beautiful before, and the more he learned about her, the more transfixed he became. She could play piano and sing, and she was far more elegant than the women he'd known growing up in the farm community of Jonesboro. The newness of love clouded the reality that they were two fledgling adults who had no idea where life would take them.

Mom expected a traditional church ceremony, but Dad wouldn't have it. I'm sure he saw the expense of a formal wedding as a waste of money. Instead, my pragmatic father talked her into eloping.

When Dad wanted something, he could be terribly persuasive. On June 14, 1947, just a few weeks after Mother's graduation, they drove to Clovis, New Mexico, and married. As a way of paying homage, they attended church the next day at the local Methodist Church. Mom kept the program from that church service for the rest of her life.

When my grandfather found out about the elopement, he wrote Fern an angry letter. He also sent Cloyce an invoice for Mother's last year of college tuition, which was promptly paid.

Despite her college education, once she was married, Mom was content to tend to the family while Dad went to law school, played professional football, and worked two jobs. Mom was so devoted to him that she never complained about how much time he spent away. Marriage and children fulfilled her. Throughout the first twenty years of their marriage, she had everything she'd ever dreamed of and more.

*W*hen I was twelve, Mom came to me one day and told me I needed to sit down and listen to her carefully; she had something important to tell me.

I was born at Baylor Hospital in the winter of 1957. Upon my arrival, the doctors immediately noticed something wrong with me.

My color was off—way off—and my eyes and skin were yellow with jaundice. I'd been born with Rhesus disease, a condition caused by a blood incompatibility between the parents. As she began recounting her tale, I could see the anguish coming back into her face as if she were reliving the whole experience all over again.

She explained that when an Rh-negative mother becomes pregnant by an Rh-positive father, there's a possibility that the child can inherit the positive strain, creating an incompatibility between mother and baby. The mother's blood produces antibodies to destroy what it perceives as a foreign substance.

There was no vaccine available to counteract my condition in the 1950s. The nursing staff transfused my blood a number of times, but nothing was working.

Fathers were not to be seen in maternity wards back then, Mom explained, and although she was surrounded by family and friends, she had to soldier through much of the ordeal without her husband by her side. A few days later she called Dad at his office.

"Cloyce, the baby still isn't doing well," she announced.

"What's wrong with him?" Dad asked.

"His blood is all wrong; he's as orange as a pumpkin." Her voice was full of despair. "The doctors say we could lose him."

"Is that the only thing wrong with him?" Dad asked.

"Yes, other than that he's perfectly fine," she explained.

"They'll get that straightened out," he said. "Once they do, you'll be able to bring him home."

"But I'm scared to death we're going to lose him, Cloyce. They've transfused his blood a number of times now. It's not working. They can't keep doing it forever," Mom whimpered. "Sooner or later he's got to accept his own blood or he won't live."

"I think he'll come out of this okay," he told her.

Dad sounded so confident that Mom felt a little better as she hung up the phone. The prospect of losing her baby was terrifying, but she believed in her husband unequivocally. He said that everything would turn out fine, and she put her faith in his assurances.

Later that day, the medical team informed her that they could transfuse my blood one last time. If it didn't work, I would not be expected to live. The procedure took place early the next morning. One last time my blood was exchanged through a series of tiny plastic tubes dangling from an IV pole, and then my mother had to wait. She prayed, "Lord Jesus Christ, with all my heart, I just ask you for one thing. Just give him his life. That's all I ask. Just give him his life."

Within an hour, my color started to change. Yellow gave way to orange, and then finally to a much healthier shade of new-baby pink. I had survived, but barely.

Mom called Dad back and told him the good news. He was ecstatic.

"I'll be damned, Fern, I thought we might lose him," he confessed. "I guess it's a miracle."

As soon as Mom was done telling me this, I could sense a huge burden lifted from her shoulders. She had literally waited years to get this off of her chest. As for me, I could barely contain an ear-to-ear grin. The thought of being at the center of my parents' attention during such a harrowing saga delighted me.

*Y*ears later, after my parents had divorced, I asked Mother one day, "Mom, after all you and Dad have been through, what do you make of him?"

Mom threw back her head and laughed her signature giggle. "Oh my gosh, sweetheart," she said, crinkling up her nose. "I wouldn't know what to make of your daddy!"

We both chuckled. Then Mom looked down at the floor and grew more pensive. "He's always been a mystery to me . . . he's very complicated."

"But Mom," I protested, "y'all were married for thirty-seven years. You had four boys together. How can you say that?"

"I know, it's a little strange to me, too," she said. "I guess I just never really understood him, sweetie." A pained, faraway look filled her eyes, as if she were surveying all those years again in her memory. "But I always loved him," she added softly.

Chapter 6

GO MAN GO

Dad's career in professional football started when the Washington Redskins drafted him as a quarterback out of West Texas State to replace their aging star, Sammy Baugh. A year later, Washington traded away his rights to Detroit for $250.

In his first season with Detroit, Dad's lackluster performance as halfback and flanker compelled his move to wide receiver. During the next four years he made his mark as one of the best receivers in NFL history. Playing along such greats as Doak Walker, Yale Lary, Leon Hart, and Bobby Layne, Dad helped the Lions get to the World Championship game three years in a row, winning back-to-back titles in 1952 and 1953. He set five individual records for the Lions as a wide receiver, a few of which stand to this day. He was named to the All-Pro team twice in a brief career of five years. In 1991, he was inducted into the Michigan Sports Hall of Fame.

Perhaps his biggest play came during the 1953 season. It was a snowbound Thanksgiving Day game against the Green Bay Packers.

"It was a bad day in Detroit," Dad once recalled, "and Green Bay was kicking us all over the field. Bobby had a case of bursitis, and our passing attack wasn't working at all. On one of those plays, the defensive back who was defending me turned his knee. He had defi-nitely hurt himself. He's not the kind of guy you beat, but if you keep trying long enough, somehow you manage to do it once or twice."

With a 15–7 lead in the third quarter, Green Bay fumbled on the Lion's three-yard line. Bobby Layne later recounted what happened next: "I called for a long one to Cloyce Box. I dropped back deep in our end zone, and the boys protected well for me. I peered through the driving snowstorm and saw Box running at full throttle, and I cut loose."

Dad never broke stride. He caught the ball at the Detroit 45-yard line and went all the way for a 97-yard touchdown. It was the longest pass in Layne's career, and the longest pass in Detroit's history. The Lions won the game 35–15.

Dad admitted afterward, "I guess you might call the long pass that Bobby threw me as my biggest thrill."

*B*ut the 1954 season was a bust for Dad. He suffered from leg muscle problems that took the edge off his speed, and his perfor-mance plummeted. After catching sixteen passes in 1953, he only caught six in 1954. After the glory of the '53 season, this must have been a stinging disappointment. By the end of the season, my prag-matic father had acknowledged the odds ahead. Defensive backs had more speed, and the pass catchers were getting faster and stronger, trends in the game that would continue for decades.

After the Lions lost the championship game in 1954, Dad retired from professional football altogether. By 1955 the Lions magic was gone; they finished that year in last place in their division. They came back to win another championship in 1957, but it would be the last time the Lions ever rose to the top of the NFL.

*N*o one will ever know how great an athlete my father might have been. He'd done a stint in the marines before being drafted by Washington, which took away many of his best years. By the time he joined the Lions he was already twenty-six, old for a rookie. As good as he was, I can't imagine what he might have accomplished if he'd started a little earlier and played a full career.

But the real beauty of my father's NFL career was not that he was a star receiver or that he played on two championship teams, or even that he helped the Lions build their one and only mini-dynasty. The real beauty of his career in pro football was this: he got in, he did well, and then he got out. He didn't get injured, and he didn't allow himself to get sucked up into the vortex of professional sports. To Dad, pro football was a stepping-stone to get him through law school, and not much else.

Upon his retirement from the NFL, a reporter asked him what he liked best about professional football. He answered: "My first thrill was my first paycheck and my last thrill was my last paycheck. Folks said, 'Oh you loved it, you'd have played for nothing.' Truth of the matter is, I just about did."

This was the essence of my father as a young man. He never lost sight of the big picture and never wavered from his authentic path in life, which was to finish his education, find a job, and start making money. The only time Dad ever looked over his shoulder was to catch a touchdown pass. There was a future that was his for the making beckoning to him. He set his sights entirely on that.

*D*ad's business career began in 1952 with an "interview" in the locker room after a game in Detroit. He and Doak Walker were sitting on the bench in front of their lockers, trying to catch their breath after a particularly hard-fought win, when a man looking very much out of place in a dark suit and tie walked right up to the two NFL stars like he owned the place.

"Gentlemen!" he boomed, grinning down at them as if it was their lucky day. "How'd y'all like to be in the construction business?"

The man was Jerry Sullivan, vice president of Fuller Construction. The company's illustrious founder, George A. Fuller, had invented the skyscraper. In 1882 he'd started the company that built Daniel Burnham's iconic Flatiron Building in New York City. It was also the general contractor behind many of the great national monuments in Washington, DC, including the Lincoln Memorial and the US Supreme Court building. In addition to hundreds of other projects, Fuller built the Philadelphia Museum of Art, the Hotel Pierre, and the capitol buildings of Maine, Louisiana, and West Virginia. These were sensational projects in their time, many of them bigger than anyone had ever seen before. With an impeccable reputation for quality and offices in every big city on the East Coast, Fuller was one of the largest construction firms in the world.

In the early 1950s, management searched for a way to continue the company's growth. When they decided to expand into the Southwest, Dallas was a natural choice in which to open their newest office.

Despite its pristine image, Fuller was still a "Yankee" company. Management wanted to recruit some local talent to help open doors in Texas, but they knew this couldn't be just anybody. Fuller was a big-name player, and it needed some big names to go along with it.

When Jerry Sullivan strode purposefully into the locker room that day, he certainly knew about Doak Walker, who'd become famous after winning the Heisman Trophy in 1948. He'd also heard of Doak's sidekick, Cloyce Box. Doak and Cloyce looked like a perfect match for Fuller's expansion plans.

Dad was hired as a part-time employee during the off-season in 1952. After graduating from law school and retiring from pro football, he went full time with Fuller in 1954. From there, his career advanced with a velocity that rivaled his speed as a wide receiver. Promotions came fast and furious, and from late 1955 to 1960, he was the chief administrator for large-scale projects around the Dallas area. My family moved from Waco to Dallas in 1956, the year before I was born, when Dad was appointed to head up Fuller's new Dallas office.

While at Fuller, Dad formed many personal connections that would serve him throughout the rest of his professional life. One of these was with the wealthy oilman, Kenneth Stanley "Boots" Adams Sr.

According to lore, when Adams was three years old he received a pair of black leather boots with red tops. He liked them so much he refused to take them off, even to go to bed. Everyone started calling him "Boots."

Mr. Adams was elected president of Phillips Petroleum at age thirty-eight. For ten years, throughout World War II, he brilliantly directed a huge expansion and diversification of Phillips into the petrochemical field. He became CEO at age forty-eight, and in 1951 he was elected chairman of the board. By 1953, the company had grown to assets of $1 billion.

In 1962, Fuller began erecting a new office tower in Bartlesville, Oklahoma, to serve as the new headquarters for Phillips Petroleum. This is when Dad first met Boots Adams.

A year or two later, Dad had the opportunity to purchase a defunct cement plant in Pryor, Oklahoma. With his heavy construction background at Fuller, Dad knew a lot about cement. All he needed was capital, so he went looking for investors. When he called on the wealthy oilman, their meeting lasted a grand total of ten minutes.

Boots and my dad were almost mirror images of each other. They each had something the other needed, and they saw in one another things they wanted to see in themselves. My father saw in Boots Adams what he desperately wanted to become: a man of legitimate wealth. Then there was the man's name; how on earth could my father *not* fall for someone named "Boots"?

As proud as he was of his accomplishments at Phillips, Mr. Adams was an athlete at heart. Boots could hardly believe that my father, a college basketball star turned NFL record-setting wide receiver, was sitting in his office asking for a modest investment in a cement company. Dad and Boots Adams agreed to join forces, and the two of them created the Oklahoma Cement Company (OKC).

An unbreakable bond was created that day, one that seemed unusual for business partners. But these were not typical men. My father kept a photo of Boots's chest cavity, snapped during Mr. Adams's open-heart surgery, hanging in a prominent location in his office. Boots had scrawled a handwritten note to Dad at the top. As a kid I'd pass by it and think it was gross, but now I see it differently. What Boots was revealing, perhaps unwittingly, was his complete faith and trust in my father. Over the next seventeen years they became more than friends and trusted business partners. They were like father and son.

*A*nother important connection Dad made during the Fuller era was with the great real estate mogul Trammell Crow. Doak Walker introduced them as they stood near the construction entrance to the Dallas Furniture Mart.

Trammell Crow was born and raised in Dallas. He started out

as an accountant. He passed the CPA exam in 1938 and accepted a job with Ernst & Young as an auditor. At age thirty-three, he began his career in real estate by designing and building space specifically tailored to his clients' needs—a novel concept at the time. While partnering with business leaders like John Stemmons, Crow became the largest builder of warehouse space in the Trinity River Industrial District in Dallas. In the 1950s and 1960s, Crow developed the major merchandise marts of Dallas, including the Dallas Design District, the Dallas Trade Mart, Dallas Market Hall, Dallas Apparel Mart, and Dallas World Trade Center.

Other Crow developments included properties in Brussels, Hong Kong, San Francisco, Miami, Washington DC, Houston, Atlanta, Kansas City, and Minneapolis among many others. Crow founded the Trammell Crow Company, Trammell Crow Residential, and the Wyndham Hotel Company.

During the mid-sixties, my father and Mr. Crow put together the CBS Realty group (which stood for Crow, Box, and Sussman) for the purpose of building a ten-story office building at 1949 North Stemmons Freeway in Dallas. The top two floors would become the office for the George A. Fuller Dallas division and serve as the anchor tenant for this project. As a kid, my three brothers and I would often visit our father's office and peer down from the tenth floor at the old P. C. Cobb Stadium, which was later torn down and redeveloped by the Crow Family as the Dallas Infomart.

Even though Cloyce and Trammell went on to become great friends as well as monumental business partners, they always seemed like strange bedfellows to me. Personality-wise, they seemed direct opposites. Cloyce, who carried himself with the stern bearing of a marine officer, tended to be irrepressibly serious. Trammell Crow, on the other hand, struck me as highly eclectic and somewhat playful.

I once had a meeting with Mr. Crow. During the course of our short conversation, the topic of my father's health came up. I shared with him my private concerns about my father's high blood pressure, and he offered me some advice.

"Oh, I know how to fix that."

"How is that, Mr. Crow?"

"Meditation," Trammell said matter-of-factly. "Your father needs to learn meditation. I do it all the time."

"Really?" I hadn't come prepared for a meeting with Mr. Crow to talk about meditation. "Well, that's interesting, I wish you would tell him about that."

Mr. Crow gave me a dismissive smile and said, "Oh, I don't think he'd listen to me."

"Oh, I think he would listen to you, Mr. Crow—I think he would."

Mr. Crow loved poetry. As a child, his father would give him a nickel for every poem he memorized. He even published a ring-bound booklet of his favorite poems, prayers, and scriptures in honor of his mother and father, titled *This Time* . . . On the inside back flap of that booklet is a poem that Trammell himself authored:

> There must always, always be a burn in your hearts to achieve.
>   In the quiet of your solitude, close your eyes, bow your head,
> grit your teeth, clench your fists,
>   Ache in your heart, vow and dedicate yourself to achieve,
> to achieve.

I don't know if this is what Mr. Crow meant when he spoke of meditation—probably not. But it seems to explain why there was such a strong bond between these two men. Cloyce's life seemed the perfect embodiment of Mr. Crow's not-so-secret mantra.

$\mathcal{S}$oon, a large portion of Crow's construction work was under contract with Fuller. Mr. Crow (who according to Forbes had a net worth of approximately $40 million at that time) was more than just a good customer. Due to his enormous wealth and personal charisma, he wielded great influence at Fuller, and there can be little doubt that Cloyce's ascension at Fuller was due in large part to his relationship with Trammell Crow.

By 1962, with Mr. Crow's backing, Dad was a vice president of Fuller Construction and was also on the board of directors, poised to take over the top job. His meteoric rise at Fuller was every bit as dazzling as his All-Pro career in football had been. At just thirty-nine years old, Dad was on his way to the top.

If Cloyce Box was anything, he was a leader of the first order. Most people in his position might have been satisfied to climb the corporate ladder all the way up, collect a handsome salary, and then ease off into retirement. This wasn't my father's style. He wasn't one to sit back. He didn't know how to do things the easy way. After achieving so much so young, he aimed even higher.

Dad didn't want to just work for a company—he wanted to *own* one.

Chapter 7

THE PILL

Rather ironically for a couple with four children, the birth control pill had an enormous impact on our family. By the mid-sixties, 2.3 million women had prescriptions for the pill. It radically changed society and indirectly altered the course of my life as well.

My father received an inside stock tip about a company to which the FDA was about to grant approval to sell the over-the-counter version of the pill. Dad borrowed the money to purchase ten thousand dollars' worth of stock and then waited for the news to be released. Sure enough, the stock soared. Dad sold his shares the next day, paid off the loan, and made over half a million dollars—the equivalent of over three and a half million dollars today.

This was more money than any farm boy from Jonesboro could ever imagine. Yet when Dad became a wealthy man overnight, he knew just what to do with his fortune.

In April of 1965, he paid $250,000 for a two-hundred-acre ranch in Frisco, Texas. Later on, he acquired other acreage for a total of one thousand acres. The centerpiece of the ranch was a fourteen-thousand-square-foot, four-bedroom mansion designed by renowned architect John Astin Perkins. Built in 1941, it was a replica of Tara, the fictional Old South plantation house in *Gone with the Wind*. The winding road from the main gate was flanked on both sides by mature live oak trees, which created a dramatic canopied passageway up to the big house.

Moving to the ranch was all about one thing: horses. From his earliest days growing up on an impoverished farm, Dad understood that only wealthy people could afford them, which made him want to own them even more. I am confident that Mother had little say in the decision to move the family to the country and away from the comfort and convenience of our Dallas suburb on Park Lane. It made her life as caretaker of four young boys a lot harder. But Mom wasn't the kind of woman to pursue her own agenda. She was content to support the plans and visions of her successful husband. From the moment Dad had first studied the real estate listing for the ranch in Frisco, she'd seen the gleam in his eye, and she knew him well enough to know that this was his dream. Her job as his wife was to help him make it come true.

Despite its grand appearance, the big house was not a particularly comfortable place to live. Although the interior showcased a number of dazzling features such as crystal chandeliers, hardwood pecan floors, a winding staircase, and hand-carved wood paneling, when we first moved in it was run down and rather dilapidated. It seemed as if the previous owners had simply run out of money to maintain it.

For the first several years, there was no central air conditioning. The house only had two window units, nowhere near adequate to cool the fourteen-thousand-square-foot space. Most nights the French doors to our bedrooms were left open to welcome in whatever little breeze stirred outside. Electric fans whirred continuously.

The sewage system was on a septic tank, our water supplied by a 1,200-foot "woodbine" well. The electrical system was unreliable.

Even a mild windstorm would knock out power to the main house. Mom stashed flashlights and candles everywhere, as we never knew when the next blackout might occur.

Dad didn't have the money to refurbish anything more than the kitchen, so for the first ten years much of the interior décor was drab and outdated. Later on, he bought all of the benefits of living in the country with none of the earlier privation. He created his own kingdom, replete with ranch hands and household staff, all of whom resided on the premises. Standing out on the front porch of the house, he could look around and know with satisfaction that every-thing, in every direction as far as he could see, belonged to him.

*E*very young boy dreams of playing cowboy. My brothers and I got to live it. We had to work on the ranch every summer until we went away to college. I got my first ranch hand job at the age of eight and made $5.50 a week. Although summers were hot and the work was hard, it was a good job and I was proud of the money I made.

Don was fifteen when we moved to the ranch, and he wasn't interested in horses. Thirteen-year-old Gary had developed an early love for hot rods and girls, so he never embraced life on the ranch that much either. Thus learning to ride and round up cattle was a job largely left to Tommy and me, along with our cousin Jimmy.

During those early years, we were happy on the ranch, and when we weren't in school, Tom and I would dare each other to stunt-ride horses and help each other with the crack-of-dawn cattle herding. Dad was a CEO and too busy to supervise our work, so he hired full-time foremen to manage the ranch. The foremen who came to work for us (most of whom moved onto the ranch with their families) were laid-back country guys, and for the most part, the work was hard but fun.

When the holidays rolled around, Dad would give our ranch hands a much-deserved day or two off. My brothers and I would then have to feed cattle in the cold of winter. We had plenty of trucks to do the job, which the workers normally used. But when it was just my brothers and me, Dad preferred to hitch a team of horses to a flatbed wagon. The harder something was, the more he seemed to enjoy it.

My brothers and I couldn't help but notice how much more difficult the work was on the occasional days when Dad would help out on the ranch. Perhaps because of his hardscrabble upbringing, he seemed to welcome adversity wherever he could find it, and if there was none to be found, he was good at coming up with some.

The older and wealthier my father became, the more difficult he was to work for. It reminds me of something he once wrote to his mother while he was stationed in Beijing as a marine: "I seem to be getting harder and harder to get along with . . . nothing that anybody does ever seems to please me."

Dad wanted his ranch maintained like a military barracks. He demanded every piece of tack be in its proper place at all times. If a shovel was left outside, he'd raise hell about it.

The slightest thing might cause him to go off on one of us. Since the day when he'd spanked me, my fear of him had grown, and I'd finally decided that the only way to deal with him was to avoid him. I got to the point where I didn't want anything to do with horses or barns or tractors. I didn't want to upset him by stripping a gear on a tractor, putting a horse in the wrong stall, or using the wrong saddle. I didn't even want to ride anymore for fear of disturbing the order of meticulously hung bridles and saddles and shanks. If I did something wrong, I was afraid Dad would let me have it.

*W*ith the purchase of the ranch, Dad also made good on a promise he'd made to his mother years ago. Although he never said so, it must have pained my father to see his family torn apart. He felt such a strong sense of loyalty and duty that he vowed to Zelma he would always take care of her and his siblings. Throughout college and his time in the marines, he had sent money home to help cover expenses. Now he could do so much more.

A year or two after we moved to Frisco, Dad's older sister Jan and her son Jimmy moved into one of the guesthouses on the ranch. I was delighted when Aunt Jan and Jimmy came to live with us. Cousin Jimmy, who was between Gary and Tommy in age, became like another brother to me and often helped Tommy and me with the ranch work.

Trained as a nurse, Aunt Jan was an extremely smart woman with an equally sharp tongue. In a different time, she might have been a doctor. She was sweet and affectionate to all of us kids, but her relationship with Dad was a different story.

Unlike most everyone else in his world, Aunt Jan had no fear of our father. She was one of the few—perhaps the only person I ever knew—who could talk back to him and get away with it. Sometimes Aunt Jan and Dad would feud over the smallest things. They once got into an argument over a tire gauge. Dad asked Aunt Jan to check the pressure on a tire that looked low to him. She reported that the tire was fine. Dad dismissed her report, insinuating that she must not know how to properly read a tire gauge. Aunt Jan fired back, "I don't need you to tell me how to read a tire gauge; I've been reading tire gauges all my life." It took weeks for their relationship to return to normal.

My grandmother Zelma also moved onto the ranch. She took up residence in one of the small guesthouses. The combination of her lifelong battle with tuberculosis, an outspoken personality, and her perpetual embitterment at her husband's abandonment left her cantankerous during the years she came to live with us. Similar to Dad and Aunt Jan in temperament, the slightest thing might set her off. Dad once aptly described her as a person who "never had a good day in her life."

I was nevertheless fond of Zelma because she was my grandmother. I felt sorry for her and visited her often, thinking that I could cheer her up. Every time I'd walk into her house, I'd find her in the same spot. She had a big rocking chair that she positioned right up next to a window. From there she could peer out and monitor the activities of the ranch: who was working and who was slacking. Grandma Zelma made it her business to keep tabs on as much activity as her health permitted. She considered it part of her duty to keep a watchful eye out. I think she liked her role as sentinel of the ranch.

She also liked to dip snuff. It gave her tiny house an awful odor. An old coffee can that sat on the floor next to her rocking chair served as her spittoon. She'd reach down, pick up the coffee can, and spit into it. But the spewing action irritated her terrible chronic cough, and for the next several minutes you'd have to endure her hacking. I was sometimes afraid that she was choking.

As soon as I'd settled in for a visit, Zelma would begin her rant about some worker.

"Now I'm telling ya, these people around here, they just don't know a thing about work," she would begin with a glare. "Cloyce told me to watch that old colored man. He was 'sposed to get here at seven o'clock this morning and work 'til five. Well, he come in here half an hour late, and then he had the gall to cut out fifteen minutes early." Zelma's eyes widened. "Beats anything I've ever seen." Her voice would trail off as she chewed over her dark thoughts like she did her tobacco. "That ol' colored man, he ain't just lazy, he's a sorry sack of you know what."

I would just sit there, unsure what to say. It made me a little sad that Zelma had such a low opinion of the ranch hands who worked hard to please my demanding father. I wondered if anything would ever make my grandmother happy.

In short order, she'd turn her attention on me as if she had just noticed I was sitting there. "Aren't you 'sposed to be out working or doing something productive instead of sitting here in this air conditioning all day?" She'd point out her window. "Can't you see them weeds poking up inside that fencerow?"

"Oh yes, ma'am, I can—"

"Well you better get with it, then!" She'd shoo me out of the house and watch to make sure I'd done the assigned task.

*T*hings got really interesting a year or two after Zelma arrived, when my grandfather R. D. Jr. also came to live with us.

I don't know much about how my father and grandfather reconciled the betrayal of Dad's childhood, but apparently my father felt that the bonds of fealty were too strong for him to leave my grandfather out of his good fortunes. Dad coaxed R. D. Jr. into taking another ancillary house on the property. Known as the shotgun house, it was located farther away from the main housing complex, between the big house and the barn area.

Grandma Zelma wasn't so forgiving. As long as they both lived on the ranch, my paternal grandparents never uttered a single word to each other.

Because R. D. Jr.'s health was much better than Zelma's, he spent more time in the main house with us. Zelma, on the other hand, was too self-conscious about her decrepit appearance from the ravages of TB to be seen much outside.

One day, as my grandfather and I were standing in the courtyard of the main house, Zelma made an unusual appearance. My grandparents were always careful to avoid each other, but today Zelma was strolling surprisingly close to where we were, only about sixty feet away. I assumed that she must not have seen us standing there.

"Oh lookie, Granddaddy, there's Grandmommy," I pointed out, pretending that I didn't know they were estranged. I'm not sure what I was hoping to achieve. A sensitive kid, I felt the tensions between my relations even though no one ever seemed to address them. "Why don't you go over and say something to her?"

R. D. Jr. acted like he didn't hear me.

"How come you don't go over and talk to her?" I said a little louder.

"No, son, I don't need her no more," he replied slowly.

As far as I know, that's the closest they ever came to speaking to one another while they lived on the ranch. Grandma Zelma lived on the grounds until her death in 1969, and my grandfather lived with us until he died of a heart attack in 1974. In all that time, I don't recall ever seeing them in the same room, not even for holidays and other occasions when the entire family gathered. If one of them was there, the other was absent.

*T*hus, after a fashion, the Box family was reunited. Aunt Tom and her husband Lester were in nearby Fort Worth with their children, so we saw them frequently. Dad's twin Boyce was the only one not in close proximity. He and his college sweetheart, L. Louise Pugh, settled in Amarillo, where they raised five children. Boyce developed motels and truck stops along Interstate 40 while also selling insurance for Massachusetts Mutual Life.

When we'd lived as a nuclear family on Park Lane in Dallas, my mother had been at the center of things. Everything revolved around her instruction and direction. But once we moved to the ranch and Dad's extended family joined us, the power dynamic in our family changed significantly. Despite the fact that he was rarely home, my father set the agenda for the family now. He gave directions and everyone else—hired hands and relatives alike—did his bidding.

Although I had difficulty understanding him, I yearned for a deeper connection with my father. In my early teens, he often traveled to South America in his Learjet. His company had diversified into the oil and gas exploration business in the eastern jungles of Ecuador, known as the Oriente. During one of his trips Dad was gone for two weeks, an unusually long time even for him. I was embarrassed about missing my father so much, but South America seemed worlds away from Texas, and I can still keenly recall the longing I felt while he was gone so long.

The day Dad was scheduled to come home, I rode around in circles on my Schwinn Stingray out in front of the house. I couldn't wait to see him. I'd been thinking about his return for days, and I planned to ride my bike to the end of the gate when he drove up. I imagined him stopping the car, getting out, and wrapping me in a big bear hug.

The unmistakable Lincoln Continental finally appeared, shimmering in the heat like a mirage at the front gates more than a quarter mile from the house. I watched from my bike as Dad's car approached, certain that he would stop at the house first. When he did, I would jump off my bike and throw my arms around him.

But instead of stopping, he went on around the bend in the road, off toward the barn and his horses.

Hot tears stung in my eyes as he passed by without so much as a honk to acknowledge me. I tore off after the car on my bike, tears flying behind me.

Before I reached the barn, I skidded to a stop and watched my father from a safe distance. Dressed in an overcoat and dress shoes, he looked out of place. He strode toward the open barn door, so intent on seeing his beloved animals that he didn't even notice me. I wanted to race over to him, but I knew he wouldn't like that I'd been crying.

I tried to tell myself that it was okay. I recalled what Mom had told me time and again: Daddy was a very busy man with a lot on his mind. I consoled myself with the thought that he must be tired from being away so long, and that going to the barn first was his way of coming home. But rationalizing didn't soothe my heartache. Nor did it take away my suspicion that had I gone to welcome him home, he would have seen me as an intrusion. The open arms and the smile of delight I yearned for were nothing more than an image from television.

Feeling dejected, I rode my bike from the barn to the small guest-house where Aunt Jan lived. She was outside, milling around in one of her flower gardens. She could always tell when something was bothering me. "Well, you look about as happy as a dead pig in sun-shine." She grinned at me and then went back to pulling weeds.

I hopped off my bike, letting it crash over to one side. "I just don't understand a lot of things about Dad."

"Ha!" Aunt Jan huffed. "It'll be a cold day in hell 'fore you ever figure him out."

"Yeah, I know." I walked over to the concrete steps of her house and plopped down. Unsure of what to say, I stared down at the ground for a moment.

"Hey Aunt Jan, what was Dad like as a kid?"

"He never got to be a kid," she said without skipping a beat. "Aunt Tom got to be a little bit 'cause she was the baby, but the rest of us— 'specially Boyce and Cloyce—all we ever did was work."

I looked up at her, squinting my eyes from the sun. "Because y'all were so poor?"

"Yep. We was so poor even the poor folks called us poor." She laughed.

"Didn't y'all ever do anything for fun?" I asked.

Aunt Jan stood up. She wiped a sheen of sweat from her forehead and took a deep breath. "Sometimes the boys would go down to the old bridge and go swimming."

"How about toys? Did y'all have any toys to play with?" I asked.

"Aunt Tom had two dolls," she said. "One of her dolls came from Mr. Rankin's store in Jonesboro. It had a beautiful Chinese face on it."

"How about Boyce and Cloyce; did they have any toys?" I asked.

"They only had one toy that I can ever remember. It was a small kiddie car with three wheels on it. You had to walk along to make it go. It had a simple little steering stick."

"How about you?" I asked tentatively. "How many dolls did you have growing up?"

"I just had one, sweetheart," Aunt Jan said wearily. "Just one."

Dad's life had been so drastically different from mine, so unlike the privilege in which I'd grown up. Even though I'd seen the desolate conditions on the farm where he had grown up, it was still hard for me to comprehend.

Chapter 8
A THOUSAND ISLANDS

Around the time he purchased the ranch in Frisco, Dad made two other big buys. He and Boots Adams purchased a Phillips oil refinery for OKC in Okmulgee, Oklahoma. Boots arranged for Phillips to supply the new OKC refinery with one hundred percent of its crude oil needs and to buy back no less than fifty percent of the refined product, which it then sold through its Phillips 66 gas stations.

For more than a dozen years, the refinery worked like magic for OKC, giving the company an entry into a completely new line of business. The selling of refined products, such as gasoline and home heating oil, served as a hedge against any downturns in the cement industry, and the deal also enabled the company to sell asphalt from the refinery along with cement for bidding highway jobs. But the most lucrative benefit was the government subsidies that granted credits to small refineries. These credits could be exchanged with larger companies for domestic crude oil, or at times even for cash. Even if a small refinery were to sell all of its products at cost, the subsidies would result in a positive yearly cash flow of over a million dollars.

With two cement plants, a dredging company, a ready-mix operation in New Orleans, and an independent refining operation that was largely underwritten by the US government, OKC was a well-diversified regional powerhouse headed up by a larger-than-life CEO: my father, the corporate Superman.

Dad's third purchase was even more audacious. Lou Crandall, the chairman of the board of Fuller Construction and father-in-law of Bill Lawson, one of Dad's business partners, was ready to retire. He wanted my father to take over for him, which meant that my father would have to move to New York, where Fuller was still headquartered. Dad enjoyed his visits to New York City, but he had no interest in living there. He'd just bought the ranch, and he wanted to spend more time with his horses.

To solve the problem, Dad told Crandall he would buy him out. Crandall laughed in disbelief. "Cloyce, you don't have that kind of money."

"No, but I bet I can darn sure raise it," Dad replied.

"In that case, you'll have to buy out all the major shareholders as well," Crandall added.

As they talked, Dad tallied up the benefits to buying the company outright and making it a private holding: fewer hassles, no federal commissions, no public reports that let competitors know what the company was doing. It was sounding better and better.

Dad took the idea to his wealthiest friend, Trammell Crow. Mr. Crow objected to the deal at first because it violated his long-standing credo to stay out of the construction business. But few could be as persuasive as my father when he wanted something, and he wanted Fuller. Even though Mr. Crow probably knew better, he had an unusual faith in my father, and he knew the Fuller Company well. Against his better judgment, he sprung for the deal.

The next step was to convince the skeptical shareholders. The plan shocked Wall Street. *Newsweek* reported that it was the first time in brokers' memory that the board of a large public company had urged its stockholders to sell out. Shareholders protested the deal in an angry outcry. A number of lawsuits were filed, alleging fraud.

The showdown came on a hot June day in 1965 at Fuller's final annual meeting, held at a small law firm in Flemington, New Jersey. The quaint yellow clapboard law office had no air conditioning to cool off the angry stockholders who glared at Lou Crandall and my father. An anonymous voice shouted, "Somebody wants a bargain. The insiders want that bargain!"

Crandall struggled to keep order, rapping his pencil as a gavel. Staying calm and friendly, he defended the plan to sell out to Cloyce Box, Trammell Crow, Bill Lawson, and Maurice Moore (BCLM). "There seems to be an impression that I'm doing something for my son-in-law," he told the crowd. "This just isn't so."

Despite the opposition, however, by the end of the meeting the four buyers had enough ballots to win an overwhelming victory. The deal was the first leveraged buyout in US history. It was also one of the first times that a public company had been removed from the American Stock Exchange and taken private.

At age forty-two, Cloyce Box had gained control of the largest construction firm in the world. Seemingly invincible, Dad was at the top of his game.

*A*s part of an aggressive campaign to promote the company worldwide, in 1966 Dad and Mr. Crow bought two islands in the St. Lawrence waterway, famously known as the Thousand Islands. The main island boasted an eight-bedroom, three-story house with bay windows and breathtaking views of the waterway and adjacent islands. There were at least five boats housed in two boathouses, and a full-time cook and butler lived there year round to serve guests. The islands offered great fishing for northern pike, boating, hunting, skeet shooting, and just relaxing. Fuller's top executives wooed and entertained clients in this world-class venue.

My brothers and I were fortunate to get to enjoy the lush beauty of the Thousand Islands. The brief years that Dad and Mr. Crow owned the two islands gave us some of the best times of our life. Dad flew us up there in his Twin Commander aircraft. A big passenger boat named *The Texan*—for Dad—would pick us up at the marina in Alexandria Bay, New York. Once on board, we knew the next two weeks would be better than anything we'd ever experienced before.

In addition to the many fine wooden boats moored at our islands, there was a small speedboat with a metal hull. It was named *The Dot*. For Gary, it was love at first sight. He promptly commandeered *The Dot* and was almost never seen again for the entire two weeks we spent there each summer.

Tommy, who was preeminently good with the outdoors, could catch fish like a pro. He once caught a twelve-pound northern pike right off of the main boat dock, which thrilled everyone except me. I was jealous of how well he could fish. Other than crappie or a small bass, I couldn't seem to catch a thing. I never once caught a pike. Tommy and Gary were also the best shots with a gun. They spent a lot of time blasting away at clay pigeons on the skeet shooting range. Don took hold of another speedboat and explored the northern shoreline, which hugged the border with Canada. More than anything else, I enjoyed the peaceful atmosphere and natural beauty of the island. It was nothing short of paradise.

One summer I brought along my entire list of summer books to read. I took them with me to the main guesthouse and holed up in one of the bedrooms upstairs. I opened up all the windows to let the cool air flow through the room. From this vantage point, I could easily view the St. Lawrence Riverway, which looked more like an ocean. Whiling away the day in solitude within the magnificence of the island's beauty, a peace came over me that I'd never felt before and haven't felt since.

Chapter 9
THE END OF INNOCENCE

I remember coming home from school to the ranch one day when I was in the third grade. My brothers were all somewhere else: Tommy, who was in fifth grade, had gone into the kitchen for a snack, and Gary was absent as usual. He was still muddling his way through the eighth grade on the rare days when he actually went to class instead of playing hooky. The rest of us rarely saw him except at meals. Don, studious as ever, attended St. Mark's, a prestigious all-boys school, and was off somewhere that day driving around in the Shelby GT 500 Dad had given him for his sixteenth birthday.

So, alone, I was happy to goof around in the backyard for a while before dinner. Mom must have heard me playing out back, because soon I heard her call: "Douglas, I need you to come up here, sweetheart."

I peered up at the master bedroom window, but the glare from the sun was so bright I could make out nothing more than my mother's shadow. It reminded me of Rapunzel. I almost shouted for her to let down her hair, but something in her voice stopped me. It was off; instead of her usual happy, lilting tone, she spoke in a listless register that drew me into the house without resistance.

I stole up the stairs, hesitating when I reached the second floor landing near the master bedroom. We boys were rarely allowed entrance, and it felt wrong to step inside without first asking permission, even though Mom had summoned me. She was seated at her small blue French provincial desk at the far end of the room, across from the stately walnut four-poster bed that took up much of the space. The mirror above the vanity reflected Mom's stunning visage. Tears streamed down her cheeks.

I froze. Something had to be terribly wrong. The only time I'd ever seen tears in my mother's eyes was after the JFK assassination. I pawed at the shag carpeting with one dusty tennis shoe like a deer sensing danger, ready to run.

Some days I yearned to stop growing up. I wanted to remain a small boy, nestled close to my mother's bosom whenever I was hurt or simply needed a little extra reassurance. But my older brothers were quick to tease me mercilessly anytime I showed the smallest sign of vulnerability, and my father glowered whenever he caught my mother babying me. She'd begun to distance herself from me, probably to appease my father, and no longer called me to her for hugs and kisses as often as she had when I was younger. I waited before her now, uncertain.

Mom patted her knees with her hands. "Come sit, love," she invited, making no effort to hide the tears that fell freely into her lap. Her tears were such a striking contradiction to the rest of her appearance—her hair was perfectly coiffed and she was dressed in one of her favorite dresses, a pretty navy print with white piping—that I couldn't comprehend them.

I walked stiffly across the room and then stopped in front of her. I blinked several times, thinking that perhaps I was imagining her tears, and then I moved into her open arms. *This* was my true home, the one place where I always felt safe. Despite the tight ball of fear growing in my chest, I closed my eyes and leaned into my mother, the top of my head grazing her collarbones. I could feel and hear her heart beating reassuringly just behind my left ear.

Mom squeezed me to her, and then she took me by the shoulders and held me out in front of her. She looked me in the eyes, her own intent with purpose. "Do you still love me, baby?" The words floated tremulously and soft on the slightest whisper.

The tension in my chest ratcheted another notch tighter, and I sat up so quickly I jammed my head against her chin. "Of course I love you, Momma!" How could she possibly doubt my affections, when most days I felt fit to bursting with adoration for her? I couldn't find the courage to squeak out the question I dreaded asking: *What's the matter, Mommy?* I was terrified she was sick. If something happened to my beloved mother, I would die too. We were bound so closely that without her, I felt I would stop existing.

"Good," Mom went on, "because your daddy doesn't love me anymore. He's in love with another woman."

Her words, raw with grief and desolation, tore at my heart. A sob built inside me, and my mother held me in her arms. Clutching each other, we wept, crying for the loss of our happiness and our innocence, taken from us by the man who had been our knight in shining armor.

*T*he affair broke Mom's heart. Adultery wasn't supposed to happen in any marriage, especially her own. Marriage was supposed to be sacred, and to Mom, it was. She couldn't accept that her husband had cheated on her, lied to her, betrayed her.

But the times, they were a-changin'. The year was 1966, the pinnacle of social unrest in a turbulent decade that saw the sexual revolution, the assassinations of John F. Kennedy and Bobby Kennedy, the Civil Rights Act of 1964, and the assassination of Martin Luther King Jr. Social change in the '60s came faster than it ever had before in the history of the world. Mother had been happiest during her days as a Victory Queen, in a simpler era that now seemed almost laughably quaint. Back then, her father, a fervent preacher, had written a book predicting the end of days. Was this it?

A number of noisy fights ensued between my parents. They usually took place behind the closed doors of their bedroom long after we boys were supposed to be asleep, but my mother's shrill accusations and my father's defensive roars carried down the hall. I huddled in my bed, feeling as if my entire world were being pulled apart. What would happen to us boys if our parents split up?

Mother insisted that Dad end his affair with his secretary, and that he fire her. He refused to do either. He had strong feelings for Jane; their relationship was more than just a fling. Over the next twelve years, I came to view her as my father's corporate wife, the one with whom he worked and traveled with while Mom kept things going at home. On the surface, nothing changed. Mom didn't file for divorce or even threaten to move out of the house. Mom didn't want to give Jane Palmer the satisfaction of succeeding in breaking up our home. Practical considerations aside, there was one more thing that precluded my mother from leaving Dad, the factor that mattered most: she was still in love with him.

Mom did keep things going at home—for a while, anyway. My parents kept up appearances. They continued to share the same bedroom, although a new tension filled the air whenever they were together. Yet the repercussions of my father's infidelity ran beneath the placid surface of our family life, creating a strong current that threatened to pull us all under.

Don retreated further and further into his schooling, overcompensating for his insecurities about what was happening at home by pulling As in all his classes. Gary began to get into more serious trouble with the authorities. He rarely came home. The one time I screwed up my courage to ask Tommy in a trembling voice what he thought would happen to all of us, he scoffed and called me a sissy for being worried. I sought solace in popular music, drowning out the noisy silence in our home with records on the hi-fi.

This went on for nearly a year after Mom discovered my father's affair. She struggled to hold herself and our family together. A Southern belle reared in a wholesome, God-fearing family, she'd never had to cope with unhappiness during her childhood. She'd met the man of her dreams and fully expected to live the fairy tale of happily ever after.

Now, Dad's infidelity had set off in Mom an existential midlife crisis, one she was ill-equipped to handle. Resting as it did on the shoulders of her restless, striving husband, the foundation of my mother's identity was precariously fragile. It seemed inevitable that under the strain of pretense, it might crack.

She began to cry more and more often. She and Dad stopped sleeping in the same bedroom. Some days my mother never came out of her room. Fearful of her growing despondency, I grew hypervigilant and shadowed her even more closely than I had before. I imagined that something bad might happen to her, like a car wreck or some other horrible mishap. I worried about her all day in school, and on days when she was running late to pick me up, I would work myself into a panic thinking that the worst had happened. When I would finally see the brown Fleetwood Cadillac pull into the school parking lot, relief would flood through me. We had made it through another day.

If someone else picked me up from school, I'd steal in to see Mom as soon as I got home. I might be clutching a dandelion or daisy I pulled from the yard, anything to make her smile again. Anything to bring back the joy that used to light up her whole being. But nothing seemed to work. Day by day, my mother's spirit steadily ebbed away. There wasn't a thing I could do about it.

Chapter 10

THE WEDGE BETWEEN US

Mom appeared in the doorway of the kitchen one Saturday morning. She looked wan, but she was dressed. Her hair had been washed and set. My panic eased. She must be feeling better. Two suitcases rested beside her.

"I have to go away for a while, sweetheart," she said calmly. Her demeanor reassured me, even though I didn't want her to leave. "Right now I need a little rest. Aunt Jan's found me someplace where I can get my strength back again. I love you, and I'll be back as soon as I can."

Mom managed a rueful smile, tears welling up in her eyes. Aunt Jan, dressed in her nurse's uniform, bustled into the room. She picked up Mom's suitcase and escorted her out to the waiting car. I followed after them and watched as the car drove off from the ranch.

I ran back upstairs to Don's bedroom. A racing fanatic, he was lying on his bed reading *Car and Driver*.

"Momma's left. She's gone somewhere to rest," I announced to Don from the doorway of his bedroom. I watched to see how he'd take this news. Mom had seemed so calm when she left, but she'd given no promise of when she'd be back. I was hoping that Don would provide me with some words of encouragement.

He sat up in bed and snorted as if this was the biggest load of bull he'd ever heard. "I know what that's all about. She's just getting old."

I was too young to understand that Don believed our mother was suffering from menopause. He was wrong. Mother was only forty-one at the time. Her problem wasn't her age; her problem was depression. But mental illness was as taboo as divorce back then, so "needing a rest" became the family euphemism for Mom checking into a mental hospital in Galveston, over four hours' drive from the ranch.

When Mom went into the hospital, I was surprised to discover that the pervasive dread I'd been living with eased. My parents had finally taken some action. They were no longer arguing late into the night. I hoped that Mom would get well and that we could go back to being the happy family I longed for, the one we had been not so long ago on Park Lane.

My mother received a variety of treatments for clinical depression, including ECT—electroconvulsive therapy (aka "electroshock"). My brothers and I made half a dozen trips down to the hospital, situated near the beach, to visit her. The first time we went, I had trouble sleeping the night before. I hadn't seen Mom in several weeks, although I'd been writing her letters telling her how much I loved her and that I hadn't seen anyone beautiful since she'd left. She sent back two- or three-line answers, assuring me that she missed me too and that she was doing her best to come home as soon as possible.

When my brothers and I arrived at the hospital for that first visit, we were told to wait outside. It was a surprisingly cold day in March. The wind blew hard off the water, and angry waves swelled and rushed the shoreline of the beach. There was nowhere to sit, so the four of us stood somberly, hands stuffed deep in the pockets of our windbreakers. We didn't talk about how we felt about our mother being hospitalized, didn't share our grief and confusion on that day or any other. We were four boys at odds, angry and hurt, unable to comfort each other. We'd always turned to our mother for that.

Our visits to Galveston were brief and unsatisfying. Momma smiled placidly, murmuring about how nice it was to see us, as if we were guests she hardly knew instead of her sons. I always sat as close to her as I dared, yearning for my siblings to leave the small room so that I could crawl onto Momma's lap and suck my thumb without retribution from them.

The visits took on a surreal air, all of us milling around uncertainly until the ward nurse announced that visiting hours were over. The four of us boys lined up from eldest to youngest. One by one we kissed Momma's cheek, promising as we filed out of the room to come back in a couple of weeks. From the moment we left, I'd start counting the days until I could see my mother again.

*T*he summer after Mom left, Tom and I took to sleeping with Dad in the master bedroom. We slept together in his king-sized bed. The lack of air conditioning forced us to kick off the sheets and sleep under a ceiling fan with all the windows pushed up. Far off in the distance, I could hear the lowing of cattle. It was a wonderful way to fall asleep. While lying in bed, Dad would tell us stories. He could tell the most wonderful stories when he was in the right frame of mind.

It was the closest I ever felt to my father. One night, as we were falling to sleep, the room got very quiet. While looking up at the darkness, I said: "Daddy, what happens when people die?"

Tom, who was lying next to me, sighed heavily as he was prone to do whenever I waxed too philosophical. Without missing a beat, Dad answered: "You don't ever have to die, son."

"Really?" I answered.

"Not if you're a good boy, you don't. You'll go straight up to heaven and live forever."

I believed him. I had to. Whatever my father told you, you had to believe him.

*W*hile **Mom was** in the hospital, Dad brought his work home with him. He started bringing Jane to the ranch, too. Soon it looked as though she was going to fill in for Mom. He never talked with my brothers and me about this, never showed any remorse or explained his actions. It simply became normal for Jane to drive Tom and me around, taking us to lunch and on errands for the house. I began to wonder whether Jane was going to become our stepmother. Dad tried to make us see her in that light, but none of us boys would have it. We were too resentful to make it that easy on him.

One rainy weekend afternoon, Tommy and I were playing football inside the house. Things grew heated, and I stomped off to find my father to referee our argument. Tommy trailed behind to be sure that I gave Dad an accurate version of what had happened. We pounded on our parents' bedroom door, competing for Dad's attention.

The door swung open, and our father stood over us. "That's enough!" he barked, and Tommy and I both fell silent. "Jane and I are busy working in here." He glowered down at us. "I don't want any more interruptions."

He shut the door in our stunned faces, and the bolt on the other side slid into its catch. Tommy and I just looked at each other. We turned and went our separate ways. We never spoke of the incident again.

*M*y mother wasn't the same when she returned home three months later. She wasn't as sad as before, but something was missing, as if part of her had been permanently damaged or erased. Mom no longer got excited about anything. She still seemed depressed to me. Once she was back, she put up a good front and carried on the best she could, but she seemed the epitome of her name—Fern: a delicate plant.

Chapter 11
FLIGHT VERSUS FIGHT

Conflict was just a way of life with Dad. There was no getting around it; each of us boys had to do battle with him in our own way. Each one of us had our own ways of coping with him, most of which turned out disastrously.

As a teenager, Don tried to match wits with him. My oldest brother thought that he was smart enough to wear Dad out with his intellect, and I remember a lot of heated exchanges between them. But my father wasn't easily worn down by anybody, especially one of his own sons.

I remember an example from years later, when Don went to work for Dad. My father asked him to read a report and get back to him with comments. Don glanced over the study but didn't read it carefully. When Dad called him into his office to discuss it, he began by asking, "Have you had time to finish the report I sent you?"

"Yeah, but I don't think that guy is really asking the right questions," Don replied.

"What do you mean by that?" Dad asked drily.

"Whoever put this whole thing together doesn't seem to grasp the overall direction we need to take from a strategic point of view. The real question is not whether or not this guy has done a good job. The real question ought to be, do we have the right plan in place?"

Dad looked at Don. "Did you read the report, son?" he asked.

"Oh, you bet," Don said effusively. "It's just that I wasn't that impressed with their approach."

"What do you mean 'their approach'? Doesn't sound to me like you know what you're talking about."

"No, I thought the guy did a nice job," Don continued. "It's just that the relevancy to what we need to be doing right now should be more about—"

Dad cut him off in midsentence. "Go read the report, son, and let me know when you're ready to talk about it."

"Oh, you bet," Don said, relieved. "I'll get on it right away."

*G*ary's approach was different from Don's. He tried to talk back to Dad. But a former marine officer is a terrible person to sass or disobey. Aunt Jan was the only one I ever knew who could talk back to him and not get into trouble.

We all had to work summers on the ranch, but one day when he was about fourteen, Gary decided to play hooky. He invited a bunch of his buddies from Frisco out for a play day. They went swimming, rode horses, and had a little makeshift rodeo in the arena while the rest of us worked. Normally, the four of us boys would cover for one another: if one of us wanted to loaf, we would all get our stories straight so that when Dad came home in the evening, we could fool him with a false report. But this time, Gary decided not to let me join in on the fun. I got mad and decided to get even.

When Dad drove up to the ranch in his Town Car, he found me chopping weeds on a fencerow. As soon as he rolled down his car window, I tattled on Gary. As soon as I did and saw his expression, I realized that I had made a mistake. Dad gunned the accelerator and peeled out to go find Gary. When he found him, he jerked him by the arm and hit him repeatedly with a rolled-up newspaper. I watched this scene from a distance and heard Gary give out a faint cry. He raised his other arm in front of his face to try and shield himself. Helplessness and disgust filled me.

Dad beat Gary up pretty good that day. I beat myself up on the inside for ratting on my brother. I should have apologized to Gary, but I never did.

This wasn't the only run-in Dad and Gary had, just the one that most stands out in my mind, probably because I caused it. As Gary got older, his behavior grew more and more difficult. Dad ultimately shipped him off to two different military schools. Even as an adolescent, I knew that this was going to be a disaster. The tough love approach wasn't going to help my troubled brother. But when Dad came to a conclusion about something, it was like the fearsome judgment of some god on high. When it came to family matters, his decisions were unilateral, irreversible, and generally ill informed, since he was rarely around and hadn't bothered to get to know us boys as individuals with unique personalities.

My father believed that whenever there was conflict, there could only be one winner. This is how it was in athletics, an activity he excelled in. It was also a trait that served him in the business world, but it made him a difficult family man. I don't think he ever felt that my brothers and I had the right to lead our own lives. He had provided us with the kind of lifestyle that most people only dreamed of, and we were supposed to follow in his footsteps. Could we go against our father's will? Sure, as long as we were willing to take on the full wrath of hell.

Gary spent two years in two different military academies before eventually dropping out of high school altogether. My parents seemed to give up on him. Gary's way of putting distance between himself and Dad was to marry his sixteen-year-old girlfriend shortly after he turned nineteen. My mother, my cousin Jimmy, and I were the only family members at the wedding. The marriage lasted just three years.

For the rest of his life, Gary looked to Dad for financial support. Their relationship stabilized after Gary settled down and became a ranch hand. The "shade tree mechanic" would never go on to college, and he would never work in the business world, the domain in which my father reigned. But Dad needed help on the ranch, and Gary came in handy in that regard.

*T*ommy was the best behaved while we were growing up. He wasn't as sensitive as I was, and he didn't seem as affected by Mom's grief. I dealt with my emotions by trying to open up and talk about things. Tom took the opposite approach. He coped by shutting down and denying that anything bothered him. The tough-guy approach served him well, but it didn't provide me with much of an ally.

Growing up, and particularly in the aftermath of our parents' troubled marriage, it sometimes seemed as if I lived under Tom's shadow. We weren't even two years apart in age, so the comparisons between us were inevitable. Tom was always ahead of me in some way: older, bigger, faster, smarter. I was rarely ever jealous of him, but I often felt that I was the lesser brother.

Even though Tom didn't do much to provoke our father's wrath, even the two of them had their problems getting along. When he and Dad were on the "outs," Tommy would give Dad the cold shoulder and refuse to talk to him. Tommy had this stony expression he deployed when he was really upset. It was a face Dad didn't like to see.

One time Tommy and Dad flew down to a ranch near Waco to

check on the sale of some cattle. Dad was always in a hurry, which was one of the reasons he loved to fly so much. His twin-engine Beechcraft Bonanza could cruise at 180 knots.

Once Dad had finished his business at the ranch, he and Tommy drove back to the tiny airport in McGregor, Texas, so they could fly back home to Dad's hangar at Addison Airport in Dallas. Dad parked the car and told Tommy to go put their bags in the plane while he filled out some paperwork. Tommy went around the corner but quickly returned, bags still in hand.

"Dad, where did you say the plane was parked?" Tom asked his father.

"Around the corner," Dad said.

Tommy dutifully went to look for the plane again, but he came back a second time. "There's no airplane out there."

Dad made an exasperated sound. "Goddammit, you mean to tell me you don't know what an airplane looks like? What the hell's wrong with you? Now go put these bags in the plane, son!"

Tom went around the corner a third time. Returning once again, he said, "Dad, I'm sorry to tell you this, but there's no airplane out there. Come look for yourself."

Dad slammed down the paperwork in disgust. He and Tommy hustled around the corner, and then Dad stopped in his tracks.

"Well, I'll be a sonofabitch if some lousy bastard hasn't stolen my airplane," he said.

On the two-hour drive back home, Tom gave Dad the silent treatment, knowing full well that no apology was in the offing.

*A*fter our older brothers left home, Tommy and I grew very close. He and I were the only two who'd attended school together. This had a major impact on our relationship. Just two grades apart in school, we played on many of the same sports teams. Tommy was a good athlete and I looked up to him.

Tom got his driver's license first and soon began driving us back and forth to school. We spent a lot of time in the car going up and down Preston Road, where we'd talk about what was going on at school, who we liked, and who we didn't. Tom became a bit of a father figure to me, and I looked up to him with the same kind of adoration that I'd once felt for Dad.

Despite his domineering approach to parenting, my father and I didn't have many problems getting along during my teenage years. I'd learned from my older brothers that taking Dad on was a pointless endeavor. None of them had ever gained anything by trying to stand up to Dad. Therefore, I chose "flight" over "fight" and gave my volatile father a wide berth. I kept to myself and sought solace in things I enjoyed, like watching television and listening to music.

One summer evening in 1972, Gary and his young wife drove me down to the Cotton Bowl to see my first-ever concert, Three Dog Night. Wilson Pickett had a popular song, "Mustang Sally," out then. Gary had his first sports car, a brand-new, baby blue Ford Mustang. Gary's wife was named Sally, so we all joked that the song must have been written for her.

When Three Dog Night took the stage, I came alive in a way that I'd never felt before. The experience had nothing to do with drugs or alcohol. I was barely a teenager, and the "high" that came over me was entirely from the music. I couldn't get enough of it. The group stormed through one hit after another, including "Joy to the World," "One Is the Loneliest Number," "An Old Fashioned Love Song," and the soulful "Try a Little Tenderness." I knew the music well. I owned all of Three Dog Night's records, and I drove my brothers nuts by sitting in my room, playing all their songs on my stereo, trying hard to sing like them and even harder to look like them.

After running through their set list, the band took a short break before promptly returning to the stage for one encore. The Cotton Bowl audience was raucous, and the group had saved one of its best songs for the end.

After the last verse of the song comes one last chorus, which is sung a cappella:

Celebrate . . . Celebrate . . . Dance to the Mus—ic

Celebrate . . . Celebrate . . . Dance to the Mus—ic

Just as the song reached the final round of the chorus, all the stadium lights of the Cotton Bowl came on, baptizing the stage, the band, and the audience in the brightest possible light. I'd never experienced anything before like that; it looked and felt like heaven.

I doubt that Gary and Sally had the slightest inkling of how that night affected me. To them, it was just another concert, but for me, I had found a sanctuary. I had learned that music had the power to take me away from the troubles of the world and the turmoil of my family.

Chapter 12

GREENHILL

In middle school biology, we read about certain birds capable of spreading viruses to other animals they came in contact with without contracting the illness themselves. This made me think of my father. The virus he spread was conflict and controversy. It seemed to follow him wherever he went.

Like those birds, the controversies Dad got into seemed to have a limited effect on him, but a much greater impact on those around him. The incident that stands out the most in my memory is an ugly chapter that involved my school.

Tommy and I both attended Greenhill from middle school through the end of high school. Founded by a former St. Mark's professor, the school struggled during its early years. It faced a shortage of money, buildings, and equipment. Greenhill's administrators reached out to my father for help and asked him to sit on the school's board of trustees.

Dad's approach was straightforward enough. If you want to raise money for the fledgling school, he advised, you need to improve the athletic program, particularly the varsity football team. Alumni, who usually come to only one event each year—the homecoming football game—want to see their old team win, not lose. Dad argued that the more competitive the football program, the easier it would be to raise money.

Greenhill, a college prep, was never comfortable with the idea of recruiting kids for anything other than academics. Offering scholarships on the basis of anything smacking of athletic ability ran counter to the school's philosophy. But this was before they asked Dad to serve on the board.

Dad steered the school in the direction of what were furtively known as "character scholarships." This referred to a student who was seen as "well-rounded"—in other words, smart enough to test in, but also possessing qualities that contributed to the school in other important ways besides academics. It was a subtle way to recruit good athletes, especially football players.

Prior to my father's involvement, Greenhill's varsity football program had been respectable, but nothing on par with its cross-town rival, St. Mark's. Dad knew a lot about St. Mark's because Don had graduated from there in 1969. St. Mark's was considered so far above Greenhill that the two private schools, located a mere fifteen minutes apart, didn't even play in the same conference. With two of his own sons on sports teams at Greenhill—Tommy and I were both fair athletes who participated in football, basketball, track, and golf—Dad wanted to change things. He wanted Greenhill's teams to be on par with St. Mark's.

The behind-the-scenes recruitment that went on during the next year or two resulted in five excellent football players transferring to Greenhill from a number of nearby public schools. These five players, in conjunction with a solid core of "homegrown" kids, made Greenhill's 1972 team one of the most dominant in school history. They went undefeated that season, posted a perfect record of 10–0, and won the private school conference championship. The defense was so dominant that no one scored a point on Greenhill's team until the sixth game of the season.

Emboldened by his success with the football program, Dad set his sights on improving other things at the private school. Dad wanted Greenhill to hire a new basketball coach. There was no real problem with the current coach, Bruce Long, except for the fact that my father was close to a basketball coach named Bill Blakeley.

Mr. Blakeley's reputation and personality in the world of basketball was legendary. Eventually, he would make the leap into pro ball as head coach of the Dallas Chaparrals, the predecessor to the Dallas Mavericks. In the early 1970s, however, Mr. Blakeley was in between jobs. He had an athletic son at Greenhill who was close friends with Tommy, and Mr. Blakeley and Dad had met independently a few years before, while Don was at St. Mark's. They'd become great friends, and they even did a few real estate deals together. Now, Mr. Blakeley approached my father to help him find work.

Dad became convinced that Bill Blakeley would make a sensational coach at the tiny prep school. He was adamant that the school hire Mr. Blakeley and that Mr. Long should either step down or take a subordinate job as Blakeley's assistant. Wounded, Mr. Long resigned in protest, and Mr. Blakeley became the head coach at Greenhill.

Following Mr. Long's resignation, an old guard faction of the school rose up on his behalf, insisting that the board fire Mr. Blakeley. The movement divided the school between those in favor of Mr. Long versus those on Mr. Blakeley's side. After weeks of deliberations, Greenhill's board did indeed fire Mr. Blakeley, leaving the team without either coach. A young assistant ended up taking on the position.

In the course of a few weeks, Greenhill went from having a former professional basketball coach to a coach with virtually no experience at all. Dad resigned from the board a year or so later.

Following the basketball fiasco, it wasn't long before the other shoe dropped on the football program, too. Greenhill promptly abandoned "character scholarships" in favor of an approach that was more consistent with its original charter and philosophy. In just two years, Greenhill went from a perfect season to one of its worst ever, posting a winless record of 0–9.

The discord caused by my father's involvement at Greenhill left me embarrassed and disappointed. It was a familiar pattern, and it reminded me of what it was like flying with him. No one was better at getting an idea off the ground than Cloyce Box, but the minute he reached cruising altitude, turbulence would usually follow.

*T*he episode at Greenhill paled in comparison to the 1973 reelection campaign of Texas Governor Dolph Briscoe.

It was illegal for a corporation to contribute to a political campaign, but that didn't stop Cloyce from leveraging his company, OKC, and putting up $10,000 by using one hundred employees' names for the donations. Sissy Farenthold, who ran against Briscoe in the gubernatorial race, filed suit and alleged campaign fraud. Dad was made a defendant in the lawsuit and had to give a deposition.

No one at home ever said a word to me about the controversy. The first time I heard anything about it was from a school librarian at Greenhill. She was setting out the daily newspapers when she saw me passing by. She asked if I had seen that day's paper, and whether I knew that there was an article there about my father and Dolph Briscoe. After sheepishly telling her no, she offered to let me have a look at it.

A ton of embarrassing media coverage followed. Dad gave an interview about the story on local TV. I remember watching the six o'clock news with my parents. Waiting for the segment to air was nerve-wracking. Several friends at school had asked me about the allegations, and I hadn't known what to say.

When the interview finally began, Dad was resplendent in a metallic gold suit. The old adage that the camera adds ten pounds was true. Dad looked more like a beefy mob boss than a corporate CEO. It worried me to see him portrayed this way in the public eye. What would people think of him? What would they think of *me*?

It was unsettling to see my father in the middle of a political controversy. When the segment finally aired, Mom and I sat watching with our eyes fixed to the screen, our mouths wide open. But Dad just sat back in his big chair and laughed so loudly that we could barely hear the TV. Right then and there, I believed he was crazy.

In the end, Dad nailed the interview, and the whole thing blew over.

Chapter 13

SEMPER FIDELIS

Mom and Dad shared the same bedroom until I went away to college. They somehow managed to work out a détente in their relationship based on keeping the family and their assets together. It was clear to all of us boys, however, that they were paying a heavy price: their mutual unhappiness. Mom never faltered in her loyalty and devotion to Dad. Nor did any of us boys. But the seeds of discord had been planted, and they were growing. Our picture-perfect family was falling apart.

One evening, Mom was unusually quiet as she fixed baked chicken in the kitchen. I'd been sensitive to her emotional state ever since she'd first told me of Dad's infidelities, and I could tell she was upset as she put the chicken on a serving platter. She and Dad were in the middle of an argument again. The only thing they ever fought about was my father's dalliances, so I hesitated to ask my mom about it because I didn't want to upset her further.

Mom set the platter of chicken in the center of the dining room table. But instead of sitting down with the rest of us, she stood there fuming.

Dad told her to sit down.

She refused. "No, I am *not* going to sit down." She turned and made her way out of the dining room toward the stairway to the second floor. Perhaps she'd had enough. She might not have felt capable of changing my father's behavior, but she could at least protest.

Dad jumped out of his chair at the head of the table. "Yes, you are going to sit here!" he roared. "Now sit down!"

When Mom refused, Dad lunged at her and slapped her hard across the face with a full-throttle, openhanded blow. "Yes, you are," he insisted. "Sit down!"

Mom cried out from the pain and humiliation. I leapt from my chair, ready to defend my mother. Gary, who was sitting next to me, grabbed me by the arm and shoved me back into my seat. "Quiet!" he hissed.

I was too shocked to do anything. Mom sobbed her way through the meal without touching her food. No one moved to console her. We were all too afraid. Tommy glared across the table at me with a steely-eyed expression that told me to keep my mouth shut. Dad didn't say anything. We all just sat there in the uncomfortable silence for the rest of the meal while Mom quietly wept.

*T*his incident was never openly discussed. I don't know if Dad ever apologized to my mother. I know that he felt remorse about striking her, because sometime later, he tried his best to apologize to us boys. Out of nowhere, Dad made a strange reference to the scene.

"You know, every once in a while Fern and I have a misunderstanding about things," he started to explain. "It doesn't seem to add up to much in the long run, but when these unfortunate things happen, there's not much you can do about it except move on."

He was careful not to utter the word "sorry" or take responsibility for his actions. That was as close as he ever came to an apology.

Despite all of the trouble between them, my parents wouldn't divorce until much later. They had the best intentions in mind, but their decision—which left the conflict between them forever unresolved—made my family weaker instead of stronger and caused a huge rift between my father and me. From the moment he struck my mother onward, I knew that I didn't want to be anything like my father. If power and money entitled a person to bully innocent others, I wanted nothing to do with them. Dad was no wife beater; this only happened one time, and yet a lot of things changed between us after the incident.

Thus I spent my remaining years at home feeling detached from Dad. Despite all that he had achieved, I didn't like him much. I couldn't like anyone who hurt my mother. But I was also conflicted because I loved Dad and wanted to see him happy. I even liked Jane Palmer; I could see that there was a strong chemistry between her and my dad that seemed to bring even more vigor to Dad's demeanor. But my allegiances lay with my mother. Her happiness mattered even more to me than Dad's, and it killed me to see her suffering.

The longer my parents' marriage went on, the more Mom seemed to diminish. I was desperate for her to be happy. When I was thirteen, I came across a house for sale in the Sunday real estate section of *The Dallas Morning News*. The prominently displayed modest one-story house bore a striking resemblance to the one we'd lived in on Park Lane. I went upstairs and found my mother at her desk.

"Hey, Momma." I burst into her sitting area. "Look what I found in the newspaper today. Look at this house for sale!"

Mom took the newspaper from me and glanced at it quickly. She reached out and touched my face. "What do you like about it?" she asked, giving me a sweet but quizzical grin.

"It looks nice," I said. "Can we go live there?"

"Oh no, darling!" she said, laughing dismissively.

"Why not?" I pressed.

"It takes a lot of money to buy a house like that."

"I have some money. I'll give it to you, and then we can go live there."

"A house costs a lot more than what you have, sweetheart," she said gently.

"I'll get a job, then," I declared.

"Oh, no." Mom giggled again. "Even if we had the money, your daddy would never let us do that."

Chapter 14

FRIENDLY BROKERS

My mother was right when she told us our father was a busy man with a lot on his mind. Just as our home life was crumbling, so too was Dad's business empire. His fearlessness, belief in his own invincibility, and penchant for wheeling and dealing were all catching up to him.

When Dad took over Fuller Construction, it had an impeccable reputation. Once he gained control of the company in 1965, he moved Fuller's headquarters from Manhattan to his home office in Dallas. This turned out to be anathema to the culture of the eighty-five-year-old company and its eastern establishment. Soon, many of Fuller's best clients were telling Dad's partner Bill Lawson that they couldn't do business with the company while Cloyce Box was in charge. They'd say: "Bill, you've lost control of this thing. It's in the hands of this perfectly delightful but crazy madman from Texas."

At the date of purchase in 1965, Fuller Construction had a positive net worth of $4 million. By 1969, the company carried a deficit of $22.7 million. The company's rapid expansion brought about huge cost overruns, while the new contracts that Fuller had acquired to support the overhead were marginal. In four short years, the company was broke.

There was speculation that the jet, the vacation home, and the other expenses of maintaining a high corporate profile played a part in Fuller's failure. But more than anything, it seems that Fuller died from neglect. OKC, the company Dad had started with Boots Adams, was going through an explosive period of growth, and then there was the new ranch to take care of. Dad spread himself too thin, and try as he might, he just couldn't save Fuller.

In the end, this venerable construction firm that had been around since the end of the Civil War had to be sold off to the Northrup Corporation for less than book value in 1971. To his credit, my father saw to it that every Fuller shareholder—public and private—was bought out prior to the company's fall.

Along with the company went our fabulous vacation home in the Thousand Islands.

*F*uller's fall cast another shadow over Dad's business pursuits, and soon OKC was showing signs of fracture as well.

The first inkling of the fracture had come years before the end of Fuller, when Boots Adams had to relinquish his role as CEO of Phillips Petroleum. The company's mandatory retirement policy forced him to formally step down two years before the refinery deal was done in 1966. Although he remained chairman of the board, his control over Phillips was on the wane.

Not long after Boots stepped down, Phillips and OKC began to spar with each other. They bickered over gasoline prices, pipeline charges, shipping charges, and receivables. If Boots had still been in control, he and Cloyce would have just shaken hands over a new set of terms and conditions. But the good ol' boy way of doing business was on the way out. As a result, relations between the two companies slowly deteriorated to the point where OKC finally filed suit against Phillips in 1971. Ironically, in that same year, Dad sued Northrup over the dilution of his Fuller stock. I find it plausible that Dad's bitterness over the Fuller debacle was a factor in his decision to take Phillips to court. But whatever the reason, the lawsuit between OKC and Phillips became the moral equivalent of a divorce.

Oil was a big mess in the 1970s. The rise of OPEC, a fourfold increase in the price of crude, the two Arab embargoes, and the disruption of supply channels brought unprecedented turmoil. President Nixon's response was to enact a fresh layer of regulations on an industry that was already tightly regulated.

The breakup with Phillips gave Dad a strong distaste for big oil. He vowed never again to do business directly with people he couldn't control or trust. Thus in 1974 he brought together a group of his closest friends and associates to serve as petroleum brokers to exclusively market OKC's gasoline and other refined products. The purpose of the brokers was to create a buffer between him and the major oil companies. Their association with my father earned the group the infamous title of the "friendly brokers."

None of the friendly brokers had any previous experience selling refined products. None had any suppliers other than OKC, nor did they have facilities to store or transport large volumes of fuel. None of them were required to place themselves at the mercy of the marketplace. The friendly brokers were only required to do one thing: maintain the trust and loyalty of Cloyce Box.

A typical friendly broker transaction went something like this:

one of the major oil companies would send OKC a purchase order for 22,000 barrels of asphalt at $9.58 per barrel. Dad routed the deal through one of the friendly brokers, arranging for OKC to sell the same asphalt to the broker at $8.50 a barrel. The broker then sold it to the major oil company at the original price of $9.58 and skimmed the loss in revenue, an attractive $1.08 per barrel. That $23,760 went straight into the broker's pocket.

The friendly brokers were a sham.

Over the next five years, OKC sold close to two-thirds of its output through the friendly brokers. All of their transactions took place on paper only, and each of the brokers collected hundreds of thousands of dollars in profits on deals arranged by OKC—all so that Dad didn't have to deal directly with people he didn't know. The friendly brokers were estimated to have cost OKC a total of $6.4 million. The company's former treasurer estimated that one friendly broker made as much as $2.5 million during the last eight months of 1974 alone.

Despite the "losses" OKC was incurring, the company's growth could only be described as phenomenal. In the same year that the friendly brokers began doing business, net sales increased 106 percent. Net income per share rose by seventy-two percent. It was hard to argue with that kind of success. But eventually, someone would. The profits being realized by the friendly brokers were big—too big for regulators not to notice.

For over a year, the friendly broker program helped the company grow like magic, and everyone was thrilled. Dad was happy because his friends were getting rich off of him; OKC's employees were happy because their boss was happy. The shareholders were delighted with OKC's stock performance. And the friendly brokers couldn't help but be happy: they were all getting rich by doing little more than being a friend to Cloyce Box.

*E*verything was fine until March 30, 1975: the day Boots Adams died.

I was a junior in high school, and I remember flying up to Bartlesville, Oklahoma, in Dad's King Air to attend the funeral. Dad couldn't have been more gracious to the Adams family at the time of their loss. They, in turn, were respectful and grateful for his presence. They knew how much Boots meant to my father.

Unfortunately, the goodwill didn't last long.

With Boots gone, his three sons inherited his OKC shares, and they quickly wanted in on the action. Barely a month after their father's death, they came to Dad and asked to be placed on the OKC board. They also wanted to form a special committee so that they could be informed of everything going on.

Dad welcomed the Adams boys with open arms, honoring their request and even offering one of them a lucrative job in the Dallas office. Dad believed that if he gave the Adams boys everything they asked for and more, they would be satisfied. He trusted that if he treated them with the same respect he had shown their father, they would reciprocate.

But the Adams family wanted more than just a job and a seat on the board. All Dad's kindness did was whet their appetites. Unlike their father, they had grown up in privilege, and they were accustomed to the accoutrements of wealth and power. Cocky young men in their twenties, they weren't all that impressed with Dad, whom they viewed as just another one of Boots's many cronies. Their father had helped start the company, they owned more of it now than Cloyce Box did, and they wanted everything run their way. Only one thing was stopping them.

Within a few short years of the Adams brothers' involvement, a number of OKC employees switched their allegiance to the wealthy family from Bartlesville, Oklahoma. Several employees snitched to the Adams brothers about the friendly brokers and the profits they were raking in at the expense of the corporation. After learning about this and about some of Dad's other questionable business practices, the Adams brothers insisted on launching an internal investigation.

OKC set up a special committee of its board to conduct a formal investigation and hired a law firm to compile a report. During the next several months, the special committee collected hundreds of documents, conducted interviews of company personnel and others, and closely reviewed all allegedly improper transactions.

Within six months, the investigation was complete. Printed within its three-volume report was each allegation of wrongdoing, along with management's and the Adams brothers' account of my father's dealings and the steps taken to investigate them. The report was first sent to the special committee, and then it was given to the full board in November 1977. While it ultimately concluded that no legally actionable wrongs had occurred, the Adams brothers suspected that this conclusion was nothing more than corporate whitewash.

In the end, all the parties voted to accept the conclusions of the report, which was labeled "Privileged and Confidential: Not For Distribution." But it didn't remain a secret for long. After the many months of investigation, the Adams brothers were fed up with Dad's antics and wanted to oust him and his associates. Two OKC employees acted as whistle-blowers and hand delivered the internal report to the Department of Energy and to the Securities and Exchange Commission offices in Fort Worth. As a result, the DOE and SEC filed criminal and civil charges against my father and OKC.

Chapter 15
A BUSINESS FAMILY

Not unlike the thoroughbreds stabled down at the barn, my brothers and I were born and bred to work for our father. There was an implicit understanding that we were not allowed to consider a life outside of our father's endeavors. The notion of creating one's own identity was viewed in the same light as admitting some form of mental illness. Whether or not we liked it, we were fated to enlist in my father's tumultuous business world.

Gary, long the "black sheep," was exempted. He did odd jobs around the ranch to get by. Gary had a lot of trouble relating to anything that didn't have four wheels and an accelerator, and he seemed most at ease working in his garage, a cigarette dangling precariously from his lips, his greasy hands clutching a crescent wrench.

But the rest of us weren't let off the hook so easily. We were expected to work directly for the family enterprise as soon as we finished school. Since education was so important to both of my parents, it was a given that Don, Tom, and I would all go off to college. It was a privilege we took for granted.

During his late teens and early college years, Don was an impressive guy. The quintessential firstborn son, he was highly intelligent, with a promising future ahead of him—a future crafted by Dad. Not long after going to work for OKC, however, he developed an inconsistent work ethic and an acute case of entitlement. While he was extremely bright, he had little desire to work hard. For the most part, he had skated by in school without studying much. I always thought it was a shame that Don never made the dean's list at St. Mark's. It wasn't due to a lack of brains; he simply lacked the drive.

Still, his good grades and test scores earned him a slot at an Ivy League school. After finishing his undergraduate degree in economics at the University of Pennsylvania, he went on to get an MBA at Southern Methodist, a degree few could afford to obtain back then. Don and his grad school buddies would often show up at the ranch for dinner. Dad loved to grandstand for the young up-and-comers. No one could out-promote my father when he was in the right frame of mind. I called it "big-timing." With his big, seductive smile, he'd order up the "slaughter of the fatted calf," and he'd regale the young guys with tales of travels, deals, and conquests; of success, then failure, then success again. By the end of dinner, the young bucks' eyes were so wide that it was as if they had just had dinner with the Messiah himself. I was just going into high school at the time, and I sat at the dining room table, marveling at the performance unfolding before me. It was better than anything on TV.

Given his education and credentials, Don might have been able to write his own ticket in the corporate world. But he knew he would never have to work hard to make a living if he went to work for Dad. He wouldn't even have to trouble himself to *look for* a job. Dad had one waiting for Don on the day he finished his schooling.

Don's career in the family business started a couple of years before the SEC controversy began. Because OKC was a publicly traded company, the business press covered the lawsuits between Dad and the government intensely. At least 102 articles appeared in publications such as *Barron's, The Wall Street Journal, The New York Times,* and the two Dallas newspapers, the *Dallas Times Herald* and *The Dallas Morning News.* *Texas Monthly* magazine even ran a big expose called "The Friends of Cloyce Box."

Fresh out of business school, conscientious Don was perturbed by all the controversy involved in the way our father did business. None of his professors at Penn or SMU would have approved, and neither did Don. His way of coping with the chaos of his father's business world was to distance himself by forming a little company of his own. He called it Flight Fuel Trading, and OKC accounting personnel maintained its books and records.

A few years before the trouble with the SEC began, Braniff Airlines was an important customer of OKC. The popular airline bought millions of dollars of jet fuel from OKC's Okmulgee refinery. Braniff's chief fuel administrator Jack Ward handled most of the sales. In 1979, Mr. Ward began swindling funds. He eventually stole as much as $400,000 from Braniff. A federal grand jury indicted Ward on five counts of embezzlement, and he was arrested by the FBI in 1983.

Prior to his arrest, Ward called Dad in July 1981 and asked to borrow $1 million in cash. Dad agreed to make the loan on a short-term basis, but instead of running the transaction through OKC, he arranged to wire transfer the money through Flight Fuel Trading. Given all the scrutiny by the SEC, Dad thought it best to keep his own books "clean."

When the story broke about Ward's arrest, a criminal grand jury in Fort Worth subpoenaed Don to testify about the million-dollar loan. Don, who knew nothing about the matter and certainly hadn't authorized it, was understandably upset and worried about testifying before a grand jury.

The day before he was to appear in court, Don strolled over to Dad's office, hoping for a little reassurance. "Dad, are you sure this thing in Fort Worth is going to go all right?" he asked. He was so anxious that he paced back and forth in front of Dad's desk like a caged panther.

"I don't know," Dad said gruffly without looking up from his desk. Dad could be very diplomatic with those outside the family, but when it came to his own sons, he sometimes adopted a stern, authoritarian tone reminiscent of his time in the marines. "You just have to hope for the best. There's no guarantee that this whole thing won't make you look bad."

Don stopped pacing and shot Dad a worried look. "What do you mean, 'look bad'? There's no chance I could get into some hot water here, is there?"

"Oh, I doubt it, son," Dad replied. "The worst possible thing is you might have to do some time."

It wasn't the assurance Don sought.

"You're kidding, right?" He gave a nervous laugh as he straightened his glasses. "You're not suggesting something as preposterous as prison, are you?"

"I sure as hell hope not!" Dad's voice rose up in angry crescendo. "But like I say, we just have to hope for the best 'til we see what happens." He shrugged. "Who knows? I may end up doing time. You might have to as well."

Don was speechless and couldn't say a word.

"If I have to do time, I'll be a model prisoner!" Dad added defiantly.

Don left his father's office that day deeply perplexed. He appeared before the grand jury the next morning. The interview amounted to nothing, but the damage to the father-son relationship was permanent. Though he never left the comfort and security of the family office, Don lost faith in Dad over the incident, and he effectively resigned from ever doing any more work for him.

In a way, damage to the father-son relationship may have been inevitable. Dad had always had high expectations for his first-born son. Certain that his brightest progeny would relish the ample opportunities set before him, Dad expected Don to dive into his work with the same zeal and determination Dad had after he'd retired from pro ball and gone to work for Fuller.

It didn't turn out that way. Dad didn't understand that Don was a thinker. When it came to ideas, Don could be brilliant. When it came to bringing those ideas to fruition, he struggled. Work was like a religion to Dad, deeply ingrained in him from growing up on the farm. If you couldn't impress him with your work ethic, you couldn't impress him at all.

Further, Dad had grown up in an era when you didn't question authority. Don grew up in the 1960s, when you questioned everything, especially authority. Despite his wealth and success, Dad still saw himself as a humble country boy, while Don, indoctrinated by a big-city liberal arts education, identified with the upper-class elite. The two men had few interests in common: Dad was passionate about making money, flying airplanes, riding horses, hunting, and building ranches, and Don was more interested in go-kart racing, European history, music, and stereo equipment.

After the Braniff incident, it became clear that Don wasn't happy. Out of frustration, he created a new department within the company. He called it the "Office of Corporate Development." The purpose of Don's new initiative seemed to be to remind anyone willing to listen that Dad's business was plagued by a long list of shortcomings, that the company had no strategic plan, and that it was therefore doomed to fail. There was nothing anyone, himself included, could do about it.

Don became a connoisseur of fine wine, single-malt scotch, and expensive Mediterranean cuisine. He befriended a French restaurateur who ran a number of exquisite French restaurants in the Oak Lawn area of Dallas, including L'Ancestral. Don became L'Ancestral's best customer, a special membership that came with a weight problem that he quickly allowed to get out of control. He held season tickets to the Dallas Opera, and he was a popular figure at the weekly office happy hour, held religiously at the all-too appropriately named nightclub "Daddy's Money," located right across the parking lot from the company office building on LBJ Freeway.

At one point, Don went through a cigar phase. Dad had a well-known policy against all forms of smoking, especially in the office. One afternoon, Don's appetite for a stogie apparently got the best of him and he decided to light one up in his office. Perhaps because Don's office was located one floor below Dad's, Don thought Dad wouldn't smell it. Or perhaps he was trying to test our father's resolve and see how far he could push him. Testing Cloyce Box was never a good idea. When Dad learned of the infraction, he didn't get upset. He simply docked a full week's pay from Don's paycheck. That was the last time Don ever smoked anything in the office.

In just a few short years, it became widely known that my brother couldn't be counted on for much of anything beyond idle conversation. Although he could talk a great game, if you wanted something done, he was the last person in the company to ask. With the increase in carousing and weight gain, Don's once polished image of the serious, erudite scholar gave way to a buffoonish character that reminded me of the old millionaire on *Gilligan's Island*, Thurston Howell III.

Despite his pessimism about the company, Don spent his entire career of thirty-one years in the family office, never missing a single paycheck.

*F*rom early on, my brother Tom strived to walk in Dad's footsteps. He even went to college at Dad's law school alma mater, Baylor University. Eventually, Tom joined the family business ranks too. The only true extrovert among the four of us Box boys, he was outgoing and competitive. He also had something none of the rest of us had: an undeniable swagger, which grew out of his fiery, contrary personality. Tommy was hard to ignore. He wasn't the least bit shy or timid about expressing himself. You always knew where you stood with him, and people liked that. Some people found his irascible spirit off-putting, but it wasn't an act. From the time he was a little boy, he seemed possessed by a rebel spirit that made him defiant against virtually all authority figures. (Except for our mother; none of us could go against her.)

Tommy may have had even more natural charisma than our father. While Dad was a great storyteller, he wasn't the kind of man to tell jokes or to try and win popularity contests, unless he was in a banker's office. Tom, on the other hand, had a salty sense of humor, and he sprinkled it around liberally. He was somehow able to take his own belligerence, turn it inside out, and use it to connect with people very well.

Tom was a good student in school, but he excelled in athletics. He lettered in three sports in high school: football, basketball, and track, a feat that only the best athletes could pull off, and he was a standout at all three. At Baylor he ran track and played a few years of basketball. While I was in college at the University of Texas, I would often stop in Waco to have lunch with him on my way to Austin. We never had any meaningful conversations about what was happening in our family, never shared our respective hopes and dreams. But hanging out with Tommy in Waco was a lot of fun because friends constantly surrounded him.

During his nine years at Baylor, Tom underwent an amazing transformation from fun-loving kid to accomplished man. He breezed through an undergraduate degree in anthropology, got a master's in economics, and finished his law degree. Dad was highly impressed that Tom put himself through the three-year crucible of law school and then passed the treacherous Texas bar exam, an accomplishment that Dad himself never achieved.

Tom was the only one of us who ever developed a strong rapport with our father. A world-class negotiator, Dad was secretive about a great many things. This might have been useful in the business world, but it drove his family nuts. Dad rarely said what he meant, and he didn't always mean what he said. We couldn't count on him to come out and tell us what he was thinking, and if we wanted to ask him what he was thinking, we ran the chance of annoying him. You had to have "horse sense" when dealing with our father, and Tom had more than his share of it.

When Tom finally went to work for Dad in 1983, a collective sigh of relief could almost be heard rising up from the family office in North Dallas. Tom's presence took a great deal of pressure off of all of us, but especially off of Don. Finally, there was someone who was ready, willing, and able to be the next Cloyce Box.

Chapter 16
AUSTIN

I finished high school in 1976 at the age of nineteen. When the time came to choose a college, I only applied to one school. All it took was one road trip down to Austin and I was hooked on the University of Texas. The real draw for me was the local music scene; nothing could keep me away from it.

Dad didn't like my idea of going to UT. Perhaps he'd heard too many stories from his infamous friend, Bobby Layne, during his legendary conquest of the school. He tried to dissuade me by telling me over and over again that the school was full of sexually transmitted diseases.

"Doug," he'd say, giving me a stern look, "I read an article just the other day that said the University of Texas has the number one rated incidence of venereal disease in the country."

I'd just give him a puzzled look. Without his blessing, I moved down to Austin anyway.

My three brothers, when they left home, did so knowing that at least one of their younger siblings had been left behind. But as the youngest, I was the end of the line. My departure would leave my mother alone in that big house. At the time, I ignored this: I was anxious to get the next phase of my life underway, and I was desperate to get out from under the long shadow of my father.

During my freshman year, I lived in the Castilian dorm. Located across the street from the main building on campus, the forlorn-looking high rise offered an up-close and stunning view of the iconic UT Tower. After my first week of classes, I decided to drive home for the weekend. I suppose I was a bit homesick and thought it best to ease into college life slowly.

Apparently, my mother was homesick as well. When I arrived at the ranch, I found her in the breakfast room. I gave her a big hug, and as I did, tears fell from her eyes. I tried to ask her why she was crying, but she wouldn't tell me much. It didn't matter; I already knew. It wasn't just the empty nest; my mother was all alone now.

A year or two later, I realized that I was dealing with a depression of my own.

The next several years were a long and difficult road. I eventually figured out that my conflictual relationship with my father was at the root of some of my emotional problems, but what I didn't know was how hard this would be to overcome. With the help of some good therapists, I was able to make progress.

Prayer helped as well.

In my late teens and first years of college, I quit going to church. Later, however, when I returned to worship services, I found that the biblical principles of forgiveness and acceptance resonated deeply with me. My treatment was as much of a spiritual journey as it was therapy in that I had to do much of the work alone. No one else was there to help me. No one else *could* help me; certainly not my parents. The last thing I wanted was to burden my mother. She had enough on her plate. For his part, my father was far too narcissistic to admit that he was ever wrong about much of anything. Expecting any participation from him seemed not only far-fetched but dangerous. My father wasn't the kind of man to embrace interpersonal psychology.

I had a great deal to learn about forgiveness. Forgiveness, I came to understand, does not necessarily require an apology from the person that you need to forgive. In order to process my feelings toward my father, I had to completely forgive him and fully accept him for who he was.

My father was an extraordinary man in so many ways. He was someone whom I was extremely proud to call my father. But he was also a fallible, imperfect human being who was doing the best he could as a result of the difficult circumstances of his own upbringing.

*W*hen it came time to choose a major, my objective was to mold myself into something wholly apart from my father's world. More than anything else, I wanted to be my own man, and I knew that if I didn't work hard to do this, I might never be able to build an identity of my own.

I was extremely proud of who Dad was and all that he had achieved in his business world. He was a successful businessman who made many of his investors and partners wealthy. His companies created important jobs for people and helped put their kids through school. *Heck, Dad's company helped put me through school.* I was aware of these things and had great respect for them. I simply wanted to follow a different path—not so easy when you grow up in a business family.

Beyond that, I had a pragmatic side. The startling implosion of Fuller and the heartbreaking loss of our Thousand Islands vacation home taught me lessons early on. I doubted the sustainability of Dad's empire. I was also convinced that my father was a dangerous man. He had too much power over other people's lives, and I saw the kinds of decisions he made with that power. His tolerance for risk was way beyond the norm. He made people fly airplanes without any training. He'd singlehandedly wrecked my high school basketball coach's career. If he could do these things, what could he do to me if I went to work for him? I had the strongest intuition that given half a chance, he would accidentally screw up my life.

To protect myself, I had to find something else besides business, and I thought I knew what I wanted it to be.

I grew up in an age when television was king. Spending most of my adolescence on a remote ranch in a small town left with me with few entertainment options at night. As a result, I watched more than my fair share of television and movies, and I idolized those who worked in what I saw as the world's most exciting industry.

In some ways, the entire ranch felt like one big movie set. Western-themed movies and television shows like *Giant* and *The Big Valley* were big hits in the '60s and '70s. In fact, before we moved out to the Frisco ranch, a feature-length movie called *High Yellow* was entirely shot on the property, including the inside of our house. The entire cast and crew even lived in the big house during production. Even though *High Yellow* was a total flop, it was still terribly exciting for me to watch my house in a movie on TV.

But it wasn't just the ranch and Westerns. I also loved documentary television, and I thought that documentaries were more powerful than history books. I loved any kind of investigative news reports, as epitomized by *60 Minutes*, which peaked in the seventies. In the late 1970s, Woody Allen made his best pictures, *Annie Hall* and *Manhattan.* These were groundbreaking movies at the time, and I couldn't help but feel deeply inspired by them. I'd dabbled in theater during high school, taking on minor roles in a few musicals and in Neil Simon's *The Odd Couple.* In my senior year, I had an internship at a local radio station.

Broadcasting in any form—particularly sporting events like *Monday Night Football*—fascinated me. Frank Gifford was one of Dad's best friends, and we used to vacation with him and his two sons on the Snake River in Idaho. One evening Frank Gifford came out to have dinner at the ranch with us. That night he brought along a guest whom I wound up meeting and playing pool with. His name was Don Meredith. After meeting him, how could I not want to work in the same business he did?

Everything pulled me toward radio-TV-film as a major. I had a good feel for that program, and I did well in it. Toward the end of my curriculum, I worked as an intern on *Austin City Limits*. It was the most fun I'd ever had.

Halfway through the program, I decided to double up and get a business degree as well. I liked how things were going for me. I was making straight As in my radio-TV-film classes, but more importantly, I was building an identity for myself. The best part? It had little to do with my father and his world of money.

*B*ut even that changed.

During the latter part of my sophomore year in college, Dad received an unsolicited phone call from the mayor of Dallas, Robert Folsom.

"Cloyce, you see the city of Dallas has got a problem here," the mayor explained. "Most folks think that our city is the city of hate, the place where JFK was gunned down."

The mayor thought that a better image would translate into a better city with a more productive business climate. He wanted to throw his full support behind a Hollywood production company that was intent on creating a new television show for CBS. Called *Dallas*, the show was about a family that lived on a ranch. Lorimar Productions was looking around the area for a ranch where the fictional Ewing family could live. Our ranch in Frisco was just what they were looking for. Could the mayor count on Dad's support?

By this time, the Box Ranch was an immaculate showplace. My father had poured millions of dollars into it, and every square inch of the property had been rebuilt or remodeled at least once. The ranch was Dad's pride and joy. Its combination of Texas scale and Southern style resulted in an irresistible flamboyance that screamed "money" more loudly than any other landmark in North Texas. It was this distinction that had caught the *Dallas* producer's eye.

As the pilot for *Dallas* debuted on CBS, ratings for the new show soared. Almost overnight, most of my friends knew me as the son of the owner of the ranch that the entire nation knew as Southfork.

It seemed that regardless of what course of action I chose to pursue, my father's larger-than-life persona would cast a tall shadow over me.

Not long after the miniseries aired, Lorimar began making plans to produce a full-blown series. Leonard Katzman called Dad again and asked if they could continue filming there indefinitely. Dad promptly said no thanks. He had a ranch to run, and besides, he didn't care much for the manner in which the show had characterized the family who purportedly lived there.

When Mom told me that Dad had asked Hollywood to pack up and move off our ranch, I was crestfallen. But like most of Dad's decisions, there wasn't a thing I could do about it.

Besides, I had bigger problems to worry about.

*A*s my senior year began in 1980, I was aware that graduation was fast approaching. If I didn't do something, two things would happen: Dad would ask me to move back to Dallas, and I'd go to work for him. I didn't want to do either.

How was I going to break the news to a man like my father that I didn't want to move back to Dallas and work for him? Every one of my instincts was telling me that I was doing the right thing. I wanted to be the one son who was courageous enough to follow his heart instead of the family balance sheet. But breaking this news to Dad would be no easy task, nor would it be a one-and-done conversation. Everything I knew about Dad confirmed my fears and anxiety. There was no getting around it; he and I would have to fight.

The therapy process that I'd begun in Austin had helped me enormously, and I found that talking things out really seemed to help. I knew that there would be no talking things out with Cloyce Box. He only knew one way to handle conflict: there could be only one winner and one loser, and he was good at getting his way. He knew how to come out on top even in situations where he had no business coming out on top. In other words, he knew how to win. I did not. I especially didn't know how to win with him.

My emotions gnawed at me. I resented that in spite of all of our wealth, my father managed to make my life so difficult. Things would have been much easier if he had just offered me his blessing, the same way his mother had when he and Uncle Boyce hitchhiked to West Texas. But above all, I dreaded the confrontation that was brewing. After watching my three older brothers, I'd learned that arguing with Dad would end badly with nothing to show for it. But avoiding the difficult conversation was no longer an option.

Finally, I decided to grab the bull by the horns. I worked up my nerve one day and called him at his office. After exchanging a few pleasantries, I shifted the conversation.

"Hey Dad," I began, "I guess you're probably wondering what I plan to do after I finish school down here."

"Yeah, it's about time you get back to Dallas and report to the office," he replied. "You need to move just as soon as humanly possible and get to work." I could tell by the sound of his voice that he had barely given the matter a thought.

"That's what I wanted to talk to you about." I swallowed hard. "I've thought this over a lot, and I've decided I don't want to work for you."

"Why?" Dad's voice was strained. It was a tone that he used when he genuinely didn't understand something.

"It's just that I have other things in mind. I like this whole radio-TV thing. I got a degree in it, you know." I tried to sound relaxed.

"Radio and TV!" Dad scoffed. "You can't make any money doing that!"

I laughed nervously. "I'm not real sure of that myself, but one of the things I've got to do is—"

"Oh come on now." He cut me off. "Cut the bullshit, son. It's time you stop fooling around down there. You can't get a job in any kind of business like that. We don't know any of those kinds of people. You need to work for me."

"But I don't want to work for you," I countered.

"Why not?" Dad demanded.

"Because you're an asshole!" Barely controlled emotion boiled inside me like a volcano about to erupt. It felt like my body might actually explode from the years of latent conflict that had been building between us.

"Oh really, so I'm an asshole?" he responded coolly. "Don't give me any of that child abuse shit."

I don't remember the rest, but it was the worst conversation we ever had. We didn't speak for months. I was ashamed at how badly I'd handled this. I became trapped by my own guilt. How could I say such words to my father, whom I dearly loved despite all our differences? What kind of ungrateful, spoiled brat was I?

*O*n Tuesday, May 13, 1980, my senior year in college was winding down. I'd heard about an article that was to appear on the front page of *The Wall Street Journal* that day about Dad and the friendly brokers scandal. I stopped by the UT Co-Op on Guadalupe on my way to class and picked up a copy.

Oh shit, I thought to myself. *There it is.*

I only knew bits and pieces of the story. What I didn't know was that the story was serious enough to make the front page of the *Journal*.

After a busy day on campus, I drove over to Jim's coffee shop in north Austin. I was seated in a booth, and as my waitress poured me a hot cup of coffee, I started to read the article.

It appeared on the far right column of the front page, the so-called "sixth-column" traditionally reserved for scandals, exposes, and other controversial stories. An artist had done a pencil rendering of my father's face. It was a good picture. He looked handsome. But there wasn't anything nice about the article. The headline read: "TEXAS COVER UP—Why Did OKC Chief Conceal His Oil Sales to Friendly Brokers?"

Halfway through reading the four-column-wide article, my waitress returned with my smothered steak, mashed potatoes, and carrots. Even though I was starving, I couldn't take my eyes off the page. I finished reading it, and then, while I wolfed down my food, I read it again.

After the waitress dropped my check off at the table, I glanced down at the paper one more time. My eyes landed on the handsome picture of my father, who looked swallowed up in newsprint. Tears welled, and I closed down tightly to stop the flow. It didn't work.

I loved my father. I loved him dearly. Seeing his picture made me miss him. Yes, my father was crazy, but mostly in a good way, and always in a brilliant way. He wasn't a bad man, and he darn sure wasn't a crook. He was a contentious man and a real fighter who was directly descended from legitimate Texas heroes. He was also a beautiful man and a hero to so many. Now he was in trouble, and I was afraid for him. It looked like he could lose his company, and there was even talk of prison.

I wanted to pick up the phone and call him. "Dad, I just want you to know I love you, and I'm sorry for all the dumb things I said way back when. Everything's going to be okay." But I couldn't do that. Those words wouldn't come out of my mouth. Even if I could, he wouldn't understand me. My father was a great man who had provided me with a life of extraordinary privilege. I simply couldn't stomach any disloyalty to him. Only someone truly hardhearted, I thought, would turn his back on him. The article left me with a ton of questions, but one thing was clear: my father was in trouble, and he needed me now.

I had to do a fifth year at Texas to complete both degrees in radio-TV-film and business administration. Once I moved back to Dallas, I knew, that would be it. I'd never be able to leave. It would be like joining the Mafia: I'd never make it out of my father's tumultuous business world.

At long last, I graduated. I boxed up all my hopes and dreams that I'd worked so hard to achieve during my five years in Austin. One by one, I cast them out into the far reaches of Lake Travis and bid them farewell.

It was time to go home.

Chapter 17

SHOOTOUT AT THE
OKC CORRAL

When I first went to work for Dad in the early '80s, I assumed that he would have me report to him at his pristine office in Dallas. Instead, he shipped me off to Oklahoma to learn the oil business from the ground up.

When I first laid eyes on the blue-collar town of Oklahoma City, it was not love at first sight.

The combination of two big bank failures (Penn Square and Continental Illinois) and collapsing energy prices had shaken the oil-centric economy to the core. Oklahoma City seemed about as vibrant as a West Texas tumbleweed rolling across the freeway. All along the mammoth work yards of Interstate 40, drilling rigs were stacked everywhere, as exploration had come to a halt. The city had a drab and dreary look about it. And yet it was my first real job out of college, and I was determined to make the best of it.

Even though I didn't like the Sooner City at first, within a year I began to warm up to it. I soon realized that it created some much-needed space between my father and me, while also allowing me to fulfill my neurotic sense of loyalty to him. To some extent, I was able to crawl out from under his shadow. But I still didn't like it when coworkers or friends would introduce me as "Cloyce Box's son," as if that were the only thing anyone needed to know about me.

I was a crude oil buyer. I spent three and a half years canvassing the state of Oklahoma in a company car, calling on oil producers. Over that time, a group of hard-working guys and I managed to build a nice little trucking operation out of nothing. I was far from living my life's dream, but I was accomplishing something, and I was proud of our modest achievements.

For the first couple of years, I lived in shabby apartments, but once I'd saved enough, I looked for a house to rent. I found one listed in an upscale suburb called Nichols Hills. When I arrived, the current renter, a cute young woman named Ruth Ann, answered the door. She had shoulder-length brown hair and crystal blue eyes. She seemed friendly and nice and she gave me a short tour. During the brief walk-around, I noticed she wasn't wearing a wedding ring. I decided I didn't care too much for the house, but I was very interested in her.

A week or so later, I managed to ask her out. We started dating. I'd been living in Oklahoma City long enough to think of it as my new home, and found myself content there. I had a girlfriend, a job, and a nice place to live. I also had the comfort of knowing that in some small way, I was helping my father.

*D*uring my time in Oklahoma, Dad was embroiled in the biggest fight of his life, fending off the SEC in the friendly broker scandal.

To counter the SEC and DOE, Dad and his team of in-house attorneys at OKC had been taking the offensive at every turn, filing motions to oppose every subpoena by the SEC in eleven court actions across three states. In 1978, the company had filed suit in the Northern District of Texas against the SEC, charging that "the taking" of the attorney-client privileged document from OKC's files violated OKC's constitutional rights, and in 1979, OKC also brought suit against the DOE as well. In an interview with The *New York Times*, the head of the SEC in Fort Worth said, "This company has had us tied up in legal knots for fifteen months. This is our worst enforcement mess ever."

Dad justified his antagonistic attitude in an interview he gave to *Texas Monthly* in December 1978:

> The whole thing was really just an internal dispute in the company. The Adams kids wanted the company for themselves as a base for their own operations. Their strategy—and there's no secret about it, they told me what they were going to do—was to force an investigation and take the results to the board of directors. If they didn't win there, they'd take it to the SEC. If they didn't win there, they'd take it to *Texas Monthly*. This investigation never should have happened. The regulatory process is being subverted to help one faction against another.

Eventually, the court ruled that the agencies had not actively solicited the report, which put an end to the "constitutional rights" defense. But the court action had bought Dad precious time to position himself into a settlement. OKC's offensive strategy proved brilliant. Dad maneuvered a global settlement with all three federal regulators, in the end agreeing to plead guilty to twenty-three counts of misdemeanor charges in violation of the Emergency Petroleum Allocation Act of 1973. He signed an Alford Plea—a plea in which the defendant admits that the prosecution has enough evidence to convict him, but still maintains his innocence—and paid the maximum fine of $5,000 per offense, for a total of $115,000.

That was the good news. The bad news was that as part of the settlement, Dad had to agree to liquidate OKC and sell off all of its assets. Dad's flagship company was lost.

*B*ut that was far from the end of Cloyce Box.

During the liquidation, the two cement plants and the Okmulgee refinery were sold off for cash, with the proceeds distributed to the shareholders in the form of hefty dividends. But these were not the only assets that OKC owned. During its boom years in the '70s, the company had grown cash rich and bought up interests in several offshore leases that looked promising. These properties were all undeveloped, making it difficult to determine valuation. Adding to the impracticality of selling these assets was a one-year time constraint imposed by the liquidation plan.

These more nebulous assets were transferred to a new entity called OKC Limited Partnership. It began operations with only $1,000 cash and a $30 million line of credit from the Mercantile National Bank of Dallas, which Dad had to personally guarantee. OKC Limited Partnership became one of the first publicly traded limited partnerships in US history. When investors in the newly created entity went looking for someone to head it up as the general partner, they chose Dad.

A year after the liquidation of OKC, an October 21, 1981, front-page article in the *Dallas Times Herald* announced, "Controversial Oilman Ends Up On Top Again." As a former OKC executive put it, "That's the thing that totally bewilders me. That he's held on for as long as he has, and has now settled everything, is amazing."

Like a prizefighter who struggles back to his feet before the final count, Dad's fortitude surprised a lot of people. No less than three governmental agencies had been after him, along with the powerful Adams family. If Dad were a horse, you wouldn't bet on him.

Yet rather than imploding, he came out of the tangle with the moral equivalent of a slap on the hand.

All the controversy added substantially to the lore of Cloyce Box. The notoriety made him a well-known, if not infamous, figure. Gone was his all-American football hero turned titan of industry image. He was now seen as some real Texas maverick, so fearless he wasn't even afraid to take on the federal government, the David who squared up to fight the governmental Goliath. Even bad publicity ended up working in his favor. In his fight with the SEC, Dad wasn't just the underdog; he was the underdog who *won*.

That's how the newspapers made him out, anyway. He never sought fame, and he certainly didn't like infamy. My father just wanted to run his business and make money. But as a result of having to liquidate OKC, Dad lost a great deal of his corporate stature. In the end, the Adams boys didn't get what they wanted, but neither did Dad. He would have much preferred to keep his flagship company and avoid the headlines altogether.

Chapter 18

THE PIPELINE

In January of 1977, the American Independent Oil Company determined that South Pass 89, an oil lease located offshore of Louisiana, appeared unlikely to be profitable. They decided to "farm out" their interest in the lease, and OKC wound up with a twenty-five percent working interest in South Pass 89, for which it paid a little over $2 million.

According to oil field lore, an "elephant" is any field capable of producing 100–500 million barrels of oil. It was years before the first exploratory well could be drilled on South Pass 89. But after extensive developmental drilling and careful geophysical analysis, the engineers reported that the U-Sand formation alone contained reserves of 40.3 million barrels of oil and 251 billion cubic feet (BCF) of gas. There were other formations as well, and other reserves. In the end, South Pass 89 may not have been an elephant, but it was big enough to make OKC Limited Partnership into a viable little oil company.

South Pass 89 became the Partnership's greatest asset, accounting for as much as seventy percent of its revenues. As oil production from South Pass steadily improved, so did the Partnership's fortunes. Revenue increased from $2.7 million in 1981 to over $96 million by 1990, and the Partnership was able to acquire and develop a number of other successful offshore projects in the Gulf of Mexico as well as the North Sea.

As production from the offshore properties steadily climbed during the early 1980s, so did my father's wealth—at least on paper. He now controlled one public company and six private companies.

At sixty-one years of age, and with a net worth in excess of $50 million, a lot of men would have retired, or at least slowed down. Dad had already enjoyed at least three successful careers. What else was there for him to prove? If ever there was a time for him to enjoy his well-earned winnings, it was now.

But as his thoroughbred horse trainer Jay J. Pletcher once told me, "Doug, there just ain't no quit in that man."

Jay J. Pletcher was right: my father was a restless soul with a path-ological drive to succeed. There was no way he was going to quit—ever. Instead of thinking about retirement, at age sixty-one, he looked forward to his next big venture: a new cement plant.

Dad had long envisioned that OKC's third cement plant would be built in the Dallas/Fort Worth area to capitalize on the ever-expanding North Texas market. This new plant would have given OKC an awe-some trifecta of production capacity in three adjoining states—Texas, Oklahoma, and Louisiana—each with access to a growing market.

But the third plant didn't happen before the painful liquidation of OKC forced Dad to give up the two cement plants he'd built from scratch. Dad had longed to get back into the cement business ever since. He'd climbed the corporate ladder at Fuller Construction, the behemoth company that built cement plants all over the world, and it was the cement business that Cloyce Box liked best. It caused him to be confident, if not overly confident, in the wisdom of his new investment.

It was the early 1980s, and like a great many other investors, Dad got caught up in the frenzy of the times. He put together a business plan to build a massive cement plant in Midlothian, Texas, thirty miles south of Dallas. At the time, no region of the country seemed to hold better prospects for growth than the Sunbelt, and Dad planned to take full advantage.

The total cost of the new plant would be a staggering $177,200,000. Dad put up $40,500,000 of his own money—representing eighty percent of his liquid net worth—to make the deal work. That left about $120,000,000 that he'd have to raise from a consortium of banks and bond offerings.

Of course, the lenders saw a lot of obstacles to funding such an enormous loan for a "greenfield" project, and the banks made him personally guarantee everything. To appease the lenders' doubts, Dad brought in his oldest partner who had experience with big projects: Trammell Crow. He gave Mr. Crow a blanket indemnity to join in the fray. The new company became known as the Box Crow Cement Co.

Dad and Mr. Crow were required to put up substantial personal collateral to guarantee completion of the plant. Dad pledged the vast majority of his Frisco ranch (with an approximate value of $30 million), while Mr. Crow put up his interests in the Village Apartments complex in Dallas. This proved to be enough, and all the loan documents were signed on December 17, 1984, with construction on the new cement plant to begin soon after.

*D*ad might have been crazy for betting his ranch on the new plant, but he sure wasn't stupid. He knew the risks, and he knew that if the investment failed, he could be broke again. For a man who'd grown up so poor during the Depression, this was not a risk he was willing to take. He needed a hedge.

It wouldn't take him long to find one: South Pass 89.

South Pass 89 produced a lot of offshore oil every day. This oil was transported to the shore through a pipeline system owned and operated by the Marathon Oil Company, which pulled in oil from a number of different offshore locations. For this service, OKC Limited Partnership had to pay a federally regulated tariff of $2.75 per barrel to Marathon. All of this was fine, part of the costs of doing business, but Dad became concerned that future production might exceed the pipeline system's overall capacity, and that his oil might have to wait in line behind other suppliers. If he owned an interest in the pipeline, however, he could ensure that he'd always have the capacity he needed to get all of his oil to shore.

In August of 1984—only months before closing on the financing to build the new cement plant—Dad made an offer to purchase an interest in the pipeline. Marathon accepted the deal, and a purchase contract was drawn up between Marathon and OKC Limited Partnership. But at the last minute, Dad substituted the name of CKB Petroleum—a private company owned by our family—into the contract. At the time, no one seemed to mind.

The deal between CKB Petroleum and Marathon to purchase the pipeline was closed on February 28, 1985—only two and a half months after construction began on the Box Crow plant. The purchase price of the pipeline was $4.7 million.

For every barrel of oil shipped through OKC Limited Partnership's account, CKB Petroleum would receive the federally regulated tariff of $2.75.

The transaction was problematic on a number of fronts, the most obvious of which was that Dad was on both sides of it. As the general partner of OKC Limited Partnership, he controlled the sale of the pipeline. As the owner of CKB Petroleum, he was also the buyer.

The fact that it was an affiliated-party transaction did not *necessarily* make it fraudulent. The terms of the partnership agreement permitted transactions between the limited partnership and "affiliates" of the general partner, as long as the terms were "fair and reasonable and no less favorable than could be obtained from third parties." The problem with the pipeline deal was that it turned out to be too favorable for my family. In exchange for the $4.7 million payment, CKB Petroleum was able to collect $4.3 million during the first year of operations alone, earning back virtually the entire purchase price in twelve months. During the next seven years, from 1985 to 1991, CKB Petroleum collected no less than $21.4 million. These were monies that would otherwise have remained within the coffers of the public shareholders of OKC Limited Partnership. Much like the friendly brokers, Dad was again transferring money away from a public company that he controlled.

I will never comprehend how, in the aftermath of the friendly broker controversy with the SEC, Dad imagined that he should once again place himself in the crosshairs of public shareholders to which he owed fiduciary duties. But I do know that all of a sudden, the financial risks of building his expensive new cement plant didn't seem so daunting.

During the first two years that we owned the pipeline, it brought in more than $9 million cash. This level of income quickly proved addictive to the family enterprise, and we all would pay the price. What once was an organization intent on creating value became little more than a lifestyle support mechanism for my family. In the end, the inspirational spirit of Cloyce Box—the man who built oil companies, managed international construction, and left a lasting mark on the Texas industrial landscape—gave way to a passive family office, one focused largely on accounting and legal issues.

Less than three weeks before buying the pipeline, Dad bought a 355-acre thoroughbred horse farm in Ocala, Florida. After spending $8 million to renovate the main house and farm, which he named CB Farms, he created a brochure for the property. It stated: "no expense was spared to make CB Farms one of the best thoroughbred facilities possible." Never was a more truthful statement made.

From this point on, it was just a matter of time: like all debts, this one would eventually come due.

Chapter 19

FUMBLING AWAY THE
ESTATE PLAN

Now that my family owned an offshore pipeline capable of generating millions of dollars in cash each year, our tin-can trucking operation in Oklahoma City looked almost silly. The business never made any real money; we were more or less swapping dollars. Then came the mid-1980s collapse in oil prices, and our super-thin margins became even thinner.

In early 1985, I got the phone call that I'd been dreading. I was certainly aware of the new cement plant, and I knew that Dad wanted me to move back to Texas to join the sales team. But I liked keeping a safe distance from all the frenetic activity going on back home.

Dad didn't bother with niceties. "It's time to close up shop," he announced. "Trading margins are no good, and we can't make any money in that chicken-shit little business. You need to move home right away."

I got so mad I threw the phone down. Dad's decree had come at a horrible time. I wasn't so much upset at his decision to shutter our fledgling trucking business; after all, I'd taken the job just to please him. If we weren't making money, closing it made sense.

Over the past three years, I'd made Oklahoma City my home. I'd made some friends there, and I was proud of our modest accomplishments. A team of oil field hands and I had started with almost nothing and built the operation up enough to keep five trucks busy. Now we had to close down everything, give back all of our hard-fought clients, and lay off all our employees, who'd come to work for us under assurances that we would be a stable outfit. We were more or less reneging on our word. I wasn't proud of that.

Everyone knew I wouldn't be losing *my* job. I had a new one waiting for me in Texas, working for my rich daddy. It made me feel "privileged," but not in a good way.

When I broke the news to Ruth Ann, however, she thought it sounded great. She liked Dallas, and she said she might want to live there herself someday. Then she told me she had no interest in moving with me unless she was wearing an engagement ring.

I'd only been dating Ruth Ann for a little over a year. I was twenty-seven and nowhere near ready to get married. But I didn't want to break up with her just because my dad was building a cement plant in Texas. A long-distance relationship didn't make any sense to me. I'd already spent enough time alone, and I was afraid that Ruth Ann and I would grow apart. What's more, as much as I resented it, my relationship with Ruth Ann was predicated on a dynamic where she pretty much called all the shots and I went along with the plan. If she wanted to get married, I wasn't going to let my feelings about it stand in the way. Had I stopped to admit it to myself, this mimicked the relationship I had with my father.

In the end, at a time when I most needed to let things take their natural course, I bought her a ring. We packed up and relocated to Dallas, the divorce capital of the world, and set a wedding date a short six months off.

I didn't expect my father to take my personal life into consideration when it came to the business, but I thought that maybe from a parental standpoint, he would at least be interested in seeing his son settle down. His actions indicated otherwise.

Within a week of my engagement, Dad wrote me a long letter. He had initiated some serious estate planning, and given the number of entities under his control, the amount of wealth he had accumulated, and the public and private nature of the ownership structures, his attorneys had recommended an "asset freeze."

The idea was straightforward enough: transfer as many assets as possible from my parents' estate to us boys to mitigate federal estate taxes. We would form a Delaware corporation known as Box Brothers Holding Company (BBHC), which would own six other private side businesses. The shares of the publicly traded oil company, OKC Limited Partnership (OKC LP), would continue to be owned by Dad personally.

To determine who controlled BBHC, there were two classes of stock: class A (voting) and class B (nonvoting). Dad would gift away virtually all of the class "B" stock, representing equity ownership of the holding company, to me and my three brothers, his twin Boyce, and his six nephews. He would retain all the class "A" shares. The beauty of the asset freeze was that it gave away all of the equity in the family company while leaving my father with control over the entire enterprise.

In terms of my impending marriage, however, the plan spelled disaster. Under Texas law, property received as a gift is considered the separate property of the person receiving it. In other words, that person's spouse can't claim it as community property. But Texas law also stipulates that if separate property generates distributions or revenue—which it often does—then that newly generated income *can* be considered community property. Further, given enough time, separate property can become "commingled" with community property. Commingled property can be traced back to its origins in order to maintain some separation, but if record keeping has been lax—which it often is—this can be an expensive and time-consuming process.

Dad's cement plant was built with the intention of generating a lot of cash for the family stockholders—not, in his view, for their spouses. The simplest way for his estate lawyers to solve this issue was to recommend prenuptial agreements.

Dad's letter indicated that ownership of the family company must remain within the family. When he gifted the "B" shares to us boys, he intended each of us to own them as our separate property. He did not want any of the shares to become subject to a spousal claim in a divorce. I was to promptly broach the matter with my fiancée and give her the copy of the prenuptial agreement he'd enclosed for us to review.

Dread swept over me while questions raced through my mind. If Ruth Ann balked, what would I do? What if it came down to a standoff between my fiancée and my father? Would I break off the engagement? My father already had too much power over my life. Could I afford to let him take more? If Ruth Ann refused to sign the agreement, would my father wonder who wore the pants in our relationship? Yet if I let his estate planning process dictate the course of my life, what would that say about me?

To make matters worse, Ruth Ann was an attorney. I just knew the prenup wasn't going to go over well with her.

It was no use to try and discuss my concerns with my father. His directives flowed in one direction, and I had little confidence in his willingness to listen. And after the blow-up we'd had over my choice of career back when I was in college, I feared he would get upset if I said something the wrong way.

I put it off for several anxiety-laden days, but one evening, I knew I finally had to tell Ruth Ann about Dad's letter. After dinner at my place, I handed the thick set of legal documents across the table to her, knowing full well that she'd have no problem understanding the contents.

Ruth Ann's mouth fell open. Her eyes widened into a hard glare. She took the prenup from my outstretched hand as if it were toxic.

"Hell no, I'm not gonna sign any agreement!" she yelled as she rifled through the paperwork. She whipped through each sheet, pausing intermittently to shake her head as some phrase or another caught her eye. She shook her head adamantly as she turned the pages. Finally she flung the document down on the table and stood up.

"Do you guys think I'm stupid or something?" she asked.

"Calm down, honey," I said, trying to placate her. "There's no reason to take it like that."

"Don't you 'honey' me. This document is asking me to give up everything!" Fury flushed in her cheeks and burned bright in her eyes. "There's no way in hell I'll ever sign this thing. No way in hell!"

"Hold on, now." I reached for the wine bottle and topped off both of our glasses, hoping to buy a little time during which my irate fiancée might regain her senses. "Listen, if you don't sign this, my dad is going—"

"Oh I know what your greedy old man is up to—he's trying to screw me."

"You haven't even read the thing yet. You don't even know what it says." I fought to keep my voice low and steady. "Why don't you calm down and read it before you jump to conclusions?"

She looked at me like I was a complete idiot. "Doug, I'm a lawyer.

I do this for a living. I don't need to read this thing because I already know what it says. I'm not going to sign it. When I stand up there before God and take my vows, I'm not gonna be playing around. I hope you're not, either."

Her suspicious look told me that she wasn't feeling optimistic.

"You don't have to call my father greedy," I finally said. "He's not just some greedy old man."

"Listen, I don't have much, but I do have my *integrity*," Ruth Ann said. "That's a lot more than you can say about your family."

"Oh, so you're saying my whole family has no integrity. That's real nice." I was too pissed to hide my sarcasm. "I know you're upset, but my dad's a good guy and I work for him. Don't act like you can say anything you want to about him."

Ruth Ann's eyes widened into a mixture of pity, disappointment, and disgust. She stormed out the front door, slamming it hard behind her.

I could hardly believe that I had defended my father to her. But there it was: when push came to shove, I remained loyal to him to a fault. I could never tolerate anyone criticizing him, even if it was to my own detriment.

A few moments later, Ruth Ann returned. When I first saw her, I hoped we could make up and smooth everything over. But she stood in the doorway just long enough to remove the four-carat diamond engagement ring from her finger and throw it at me, and then she slammed the door in my face a second time and stormed out. The ring hit me square in the chest.

*R*uth Ann and I made up, but the next six months were filled with tough negotiations. Ruth Ann hired an attorney. I had one of my own. Dad paid both bills. During one of the meetings between us, Ruth Ann's attorney shut the door in my face.

Distraught, I had no idea what to do. I considered calling off the wedding, but I wasn't willing to allow the family business to dictate my personal life. Dad made it clear that unless each of us four brothers executed acceptable prenuptial agreements, the proposed gifting of shares could not be made. I tried to work out a compromise, to explain to Ruth Ann how ownership of these shares would greatly enrich our lives someday, but she could never get over her belief that the prenup was an insult.

A sense of failure and resignation hung in the air.

Two months before our wedding date, set for June 8, 1985, my father wrote Ruth Ann a second letter, asking her to cooperate with the family plan, without bothering to warn me that he was going to send it. Although his tone was cordial, it only inflamed the situation. Ruth Ann never responded, nor did she ever sign the prenuptial agreement.

When I chose to marry her anyway, my father's estimation of me took a hit.

Jane Palmer had left Dad's company in the late 1970s, as my father's relationship with her seemed to wind down. After that, my parents' relationship morphed into a "social marriage." They slept in separate bedrooms, yet Mom went to all the events and functions a wealthy businessman's wife was expected to attend. They still made a striking couple at the racetracks, where they watched Dad's thoroughbreds blaze past, and courtside at Reunion Arena cheering on the newest NBA franchise, the Dallas Mavericks.

Dad got better looking as he aged. Along with his silver hair, his strong jaw and cheekbones lent him an air of great distinction. Mom, who had been a bottle blonde for years now, still had that southern belle allure that drew other men's eyes to her whenever she walked through a room. Time and circumstance wore on their relationship, affecting them both with equal and opposite force. The further my father's empire stretched, the further he grew apart from my mom, and the more steadfastly devoted she became to him.

I often wondered why my parents didn't just divorce. As a boy, marriage seemed to me nothing more than a simple matter of love. While the love had left Mom and Dad's marriage long before, other more complex issues precluded its dissolution. Dad grew up so poor that money meant everything to him, perhaps even more than family harmony. The last thing he wanted was some divorce lawyer carving up his estate and possibly forcing him to sell his ranch or the business or both, then walking away with a big fat fee.

Contemplating divorce was more complicated for Mom. Early on, she desperately wanted to keep the family together. She didn't want her four sons to come from a "broken home." And even though she was deeply hurt and disappointed, Mom never fell out of love with Dad. I think she rather naïvely hoped that if she hung in there long enough, he might come back to her someday.

But he never did. By the time Dad was in his early sixties, he possessed many of the attributes that women find attractive in an older man: he was ruggedly handsome, self-made and charismatic, with a private jet—or two. But intimacy wasn't one of his strengths. I suspect he often felt lonely even in the midst of his many friends and acquaintances. In spite of all of his accomplishments, my father was not a wealthy man.

In 1982, the Cattle Baron's Ball chose the Box ranch as the setting for its American Cancer Society fund-raiser. Ashley Scott, a former model, cochaired the event. The four of us boys were grown and out on our own by then, and Mom traveled quite a bit. She also didn't take part in anything related to the ranch; that was my father's domain. So Mom wasn't there on the day Ashley came out to start planning for the event, and Dad proudly gave the ebullient, attractive blonde a tour of the house and grounds.

What started as a tour of Box Ranch turned into friendship when they bumped into each other at the Cooper Center jogging track and discovered that they shared a mutual love of running. Soon friendship blossomed into romance.

Twenty years Dad's junior, Ashley was a good match for Dad not only because of her attractiveness, but also due to her intellect and ability. The daughter of a federal judge, Ashley had been raised in a blue-blooded Louisiana family about as different from Dad's upbringing as you could get. Yet she saw something special in my father: here was an extraordinary man, a man of great success, but also someone who was lonely and much in need of companionship. Ashley made Dad see the void in his life.

Moreover, my father was a builder at heart, and Ashley, trained as an interior designer, had a gifted sense of style and flair that fit perfectly into Dad's larger-than-life world of mansions, ranches, and offices. Ashley was also able to comprehend the complexity of his business world. She became more than just a steady companion; she was his thought partner and confidante in his business dealings.

A few months before my wedding, Mother told me about the relationship between them. Once again, she put me through another painful revelation about her marital woes. The impact wasn't nearly as devastating as it had been when I was a kid, but Mom's sadness nevertheless weighed on my heart. It was difficult not to let it ruin my wedding day, but after all the hurdles of getting there, I wasn't about to call it quits.

My wedding to Ruth Ann took place on June 8, 1985. The reception was held at the ranch. It was the last time I'd ever see my parents together. In a photo of the three of us at the wedding, you can see in stark relief the wide gulf between my parents. My mother is standing next to me on my right. I've got my arm around her shoulders. She's tucked up under it, as if I am protecting her. My father is on her other side, as far away from her as he can get, while still remaining close enough to me to clamp a firm hand down on my right shoulder. All three of us are sporting a forced, painful smile.

One month later to the day, Mom filed for divorce.

*D*ad's estate plan, with all its attendant complications and chaos, took almost two years to complete. It ended up being an extravagant Christmas gift, missing only a big shiny bow, on December 23, 1986.

The transfer itself was somewhat anticlimactic, a lawyer-driven process where all of the paperwork had already been completed before Dad ushered me and my brothers, Uncle Boyce, and our six male cousins into the office boardroom. Everyone was asked to sign the management agreement. Few bothered to read it carefully or ask questions about it; no one wanted to be seen looking a gift horse in the mouth.

Dad wasn't big on giving speeches, so there was little pomp and circumstance. My three brothers and I received the vast majority of the nonvoting shares of the company that day, a total of eighty-eight percent, or twenty-two percent each. Our uncle and cousins received the remaining twelve percent, split more or less evenly. On that day, the Box enterprise officially became a "family-owned business."

Once everyone signed the agreement, my father turned and faced all eleven recipients of his generosity. He cleared his throat, and the low murmurs of conversation throughout the room ceased.

"Now that that's settled," Dad said, sounding eager with anticipation, "I've got the motorhome parked right outside the office here, ready to take us down to the construction site in Midlothian for a tour. I thought y'all might like to see the plant while it's being built."

He had invested more than $40 million of his own money into the cement company, and he'd just effectively given it away to all of us. I'm sure he felt more than justified in showing off a little.

As an excruciating silence fell upon the room, my stomach began to knot. No one, it seemed, wanted to be the first to answer. One by one, we dropped our eyes as he looked around the room at each of us.

"This really is the future of the family business," Dad persisted. "I built this thing for you guys. I didn't build it for me. I really don't need the money."

"Uncle Cloyce, I'm so sorry," one of my cousins said.

"Dad, I was just down there yesterday," I said, rushing to excuse myself.

"I'd love to," one of my brothers said, "but I have to be somewhere by three o'clock."

"How 'bout next week? That would work so much better for me," another cousin chimed in.

One by one, we made our excuses, until it finally became clear to my father that there would be no celebratory ride down to the construction site. None of us had been too busy to come down and receive our shares that day, but we couldn't take any time to let the patriarch enjoy the show. Dad's decked-out motorhome returned to the ranch unused.

Chapter 20
STANDING IN THE FIRE

Nineteen eighty-seven was a year my father would have given any-thing to forget.

It started out strong in February with the birth of his first grand-child, my daughter Alissa, followed a week later by his marriage to Ashley Scott on Valentine's Day. Then, on February 24, 1987, after an arduous two-year construction phase, the cement plant in Midlothian miraculously opened on schedule and produced its first "raw mill" product. Dad's seminal project was now complete.

But as the months passed, things went steadily downhill. At the center of trouble was a billionaire investor from Idaho. His name was J. R. Simplot, and he became my father's greatest nemesis.

Based in Boise, Idaho, J. R. Simplot was known as the Potato King. He'd built his fortune by commercializing the frozen french fry and supplying fast-food stalwarts like McDonalds, Burger King, and Jack in the Box. In 1987, *Forbes* magazine estimated his net worth at roughly $2 billion.

It's uncertain what originally attracted Mr. Simplot to the pub-licly traded units of OKC Limited Partnership, but given his formi-dable wealth, it's hard to imagine that taxes didn't play a role. Tax laws at the time gave investors the ability to shelter losses from businesses that they didn't materially participate in. The vehicle was called a "master limited partnership," and both the tax protections and the sizable quarterly distributions they promised were attractive to investors, who pumped nearly $1.2 billion into master limited partnerships in 1985.

In addition to the tax advantages, the OKC Limited Partnership had something else that few other oil and gas producers could boast of: it had the Contract.

After President Carter's decision to deregulate the natural gas industry in the late 1970s, natural gas prices skyrocketed. Pipeline companies scrambled to protect themselves against future increases by offering "take or pay" contracts to energy producers. Companies would either have to buy a certain amount of gas at a fixed price or pay a fixed penalty. Even though the company would be locked into paying the supplier either way, the price of the gas, negotiated in advance, would be lower—went the thinking at the time—than it would be on the open market.

In 1982, Dad negotiated a take or pay contract with a pipeline company named Texas Eastern Transmission Co.

When gas prices fell in subsequent years, many pipeline companies scrambled to buy their way out of these sky-high contracts. Others, including Texas Eastern, chose to litigate. Alleging that OKC Limited Partnership had somehow breached its own contract, Texas Eastern sued. The suit was nothing but a ploy to rid itself of the old agreement. Dad knew it, and he fought back mightily.

After litigating with Texas Eastern for over a year and a half, a settlement was reached. Texas Eastern agreed to pay OKC LP $69 million in cash, as well as to purchase its natural gas at *four times* the market price, with an escalation of ten percent per year. This meant that during the early 1990s, when the spot market for natural gas hovered around $2.00/MCF, OKC LP was selling its gas for $8.36/ MCF. With the annual escalations, by the year 2002, the Partnership's gas would fetch as much as $18/MCF. Brilliantly, Dad held out for a twenty-year term.

The Contract became the envy of the industry.

In hindsight, it appeared that Dad might have done too good a job with the Contract. In June of 1985, J. R. Simplot began to buy up units in the Partnership. Over the next few years, he accumulated nearly 2,575,100 of them, or fifteen percent of all outstanding units. Eventually, Mr. Simplot owned more of the company than we did.

Not long after he became the company's largest shareholder, Simplot and his advisors—collectively known as the Simplot Group— began to scrutinize the pipeline transaction (a deal that was making my family very wealthy). At the same time, the Simplot Group decided to launch a series of lawsuits to oust my father as the general partner and install their own management team. Bankrolled by the unlimited resources of a determined billionaire, the Simplot Group was ready, willing, and able to do whatever it took to accomplish their goal.

It wasn't long before one thing became clear: Mr. Simplot liked the assets that Cloyce Box accumulated; he just didn't like Cloyce Box—and he certainly didn't like the pipeline deal.

On November 9, 1987, the dissident group filed the first of its numerous lawsuits against my father as the individual general partner of OKC Limited Partnership—the beginning of a costly campaign that took longer to conclude than the entire Vietnam War.

*A*fter moving back to Dallas for a second time, I had a job with the cement company working in sales and accounts receivable. On October 18, 1987, just eight months after we opened the plant, the stock market crashed. The Dow had lost 22.6 percent of its value by the time the sun went down. "Black Monday" signaled the beginning of a deep recession under President Reagan as the US economy went into a tailspin. During the next few years, we struggled to keep the cement company from going under.

Things looked like they couldn't get much worse, but two weeks later they did.

The big house in Frisco had been taken down to the studs and remodeled in the early 1970s, but by 1987, it was due for another overhaul. My parents had divorced by this time, and Mom had vacated the ranch and bought a McMansion in Highland Park. Ashley moved into the big house with Dad, and together they went about the business of refurbishing the interior.

On the morning of November 3, 1987, no less than seventy-five gallons of lacquer, lacquer thinner, and paint were sitting in the middle of the sunroom, their lids tightly sealed for moving. The painters had gathered them in this central location after painting the rest of the house. The painter finishing up that day was careful to shut off the electricity to the room, but not so careful when he ran a three-prong extension cord into it. Two box fans and a radio were plugged into the extension cord, none of which were explosion proof. A spark from one of the devices arced across the room and ignited an open can of lacquer. The painter's bucket caught on fire. He dropped his spray gun, grabbed the lid, and slammed it down onto the bucket. He tried throwing it out the window, but the can was too hot, and he dropped it, burning his hand and splattering fiery lacquer everywhere.

The two running fans helped to spread the fire quickly. The painter picked up the blazing bucket again. This time he was able to heave it out an open window, along with another burning can, but by now the construction paper, spread out to protect the floor, was ablaze. The painter ran to the other side of the room, picked up a drop cloth, and beat at the flames on the floor. But all at once, the freshly treated walls exploded into a ball of fire, creating an inferno. The painter escaped through an open window.

Dad arrived at the ranch just minutes after the fire ignited. He and another painter entered the house with fire extinguishers, but they were turned back by the smoke and heat. By the time the Frisco Fire Department arrived, the flames had already reached the wooden shingles of the third-floor roof. The seventy-five cans of lacquer exploded one by one, adding more and more fuel to the fire. The heat quickly melted the walls of the sunroom, made up largely of glass, giving the fire an unlimited air supply.

The fire trucks didn't have sufficient water to fight a blaze of this size, nor did they have ready access to any water source. The ranch had an elevated water tank, but it lacked the proper connections for a fire hose. Firefighters tried to suction water from the swimming pool, but its remote location made it inaccessible.

I was working in the family office in Dallas when Tom came rushing into my office and told me what was happening. As we sped north on Preston Road in my car, smoke blanketed the horizon like a portent of doomsday. The closer we got to the ranch, the blacker and thicker the smoke billowed. By the time we arrived, the fire was out of control. Though the firemen were doing their best, there wasn't much anyone could do. It was an agonizing, helpless experience for all of us.

Both the McKinney and Plano Fire Departments had to be called in, and the fire was finally brought under control with the help of an aerial ladder. But it was too late. The crown jewel of the

Box Ranch—some would say the crown jewel of Frisco—had been reduced to a smoldering pyre. Every inch of the house that didn't burn was damaged by smoke and water. The estimated loss was between $2 and $3 million. The painting contractor who touched off the fire only had $150,000 worth of insurance.

Everyone seemed heartbroken, except for Dad. When a Channel 5 news reporter asked him for a comment, he just grinned and said, "No, I don't take this as defeat. We'll come out of this okay. We'll rebuild just as soon as the debris is removed."

"So you plan on rebuilding?" the reporter asked.

"Oh yeah," Dad replied in typical form. "Bigger and better than ever."

On what had to be one of the worst days of his life, Cloyce Box held his head up high.

Chapter 21

WAR WITH SIMPLOT

For the most part, Dad was dismissive about the threat from Mr. Simplot. He viewed the octogenarian investor as little more than a nuisance. His attitude may have had a lot to do with the Simplot Group's tactics, which at times seemed far-fetched and often ended in futility.

From the beginning, Simplot's strategy was to secure voting rights. That way, he could wage a proxy fight against my father and simply remove him as the general partner. But the Partnership's operating agreement was clear and unequivocal: only the original shareholders of OKC were entitled to vote. Mr. Simplot was not one of the original shareholders. He bought in several years later, and thus his units did not possess the right to vote. Simplot hoped to change that by taking the matter to court. After a trial, the lower court ruled against him. Simplot appealed to the Fifth Circuit and lost.

Around this time, Congress eliminated many of the tax benefits of the master limited partnerships. This caused the MLP to lose favor on Wall Street, which in turn made it harder for the company to attract investors and to expand its exploration efforts. To address this, in 1991 the board of OKC voted to convert the limited partnership to the more traditional form of incorporation known as a "C" corporation.

In a C corporation, net income is taxed at the company level, and dividends are taxed again at the individual level. One of the virtues of a limited partnership structure is that it avoids this double taxation. This was one of the reasons Mr. Simplot had bought into the limited partnership to begin with. As one of the shareholders of a C corporation rather than a limited partner, Simplot would lose some of these tax advantages. Thus the announcement of the change in corporate structure irked the Simplot Group into suing again. This time, they won a temporary injunction to block the conversion, but in March 1992, the Fifth Circuit reversed the ruling. Shortly thereafter, the new Box Energy Corporation was born.

The third major lawsuit with Simplot had to do with the pipeline transaction. He had asserted eleven claims relating to five topics. In September, the case went to trial before a federal jury in Dallas. By the end of the pretrial process, the court had dismissed all of Simplot's individual claims. However, they left one—and only one—derivative claim for the jury to decide during the actual trial: the pipeline transaction.

Neither Don nor Gary nor I went anywhere near the courthouse during the jury trial. But Tom, an attorney himself, was right there alongside our father the entire time, doing whatever he could to support Dad and his litigation team. Tom was much better equipped than the rest of us to understand the proceedings. He would occasionally call and give me a blow-by-blow update.

"I'm telling you, this doesn't look good," he told me at one point. "Dad's up there on the witness stand looking guilty as hell."

I was afraid he might be right, but like the rest of my family, I was in denial about what the jury might actually do to my father. I assumed that Dad would land on his feet. That was what he'd always done before—with Fuller, with Phillips, with the SEC, and with

Texas Eastern. *Dad's lawyers are really good*, I told myself. *I have faith in them. They'll get this straightened out.* Maybe there would be a last-minute settlement on the courthouse steps. Somehow, some way, the great Cloyce Box would wind up back on top.

*W*hen **Tommy first** called me to tell me about the verdict, I couldn't believe it. The jury had found damages of $26.5 million directly related to the pipeline transaction, and $112,000 in excessive administrative expenses. It also awarded $2 million in punitive damages against Dad personally. All in all, it was a $28.5 million verdict against our family.

As soon as I hung up the phone, I was instantly swept up in a powerful combination of fear, anger, and bitterness that almost made me nauseated. With all the money Dad spent on lawyers, how could this have happened? How could his lawyers let this case be tried before a jury? The more I thought about it, the madder I got.

I felt bad for Tom, too. The trial had to have been hard for him, and I couldn't imagine how Dad was taking the news. I had to get to the office.

When I arrived, I found Dad sitting behind his desk, quietly reading in the fading light of an autumn afternoon. As I pulled up a chair, he looked up, smiled at me, and said, "Say, Doug, how's Alissa doing?"

I was taken aback by this question. "She's fine. I saw her earlier today."

"How old is she now? Five?"

"Yeah, she's five." I couldn't believe his composure. Here he was, making conversation like it was just another day. "Alissa's fine, Dad, but I'm worried about you."

"Oh no," he chuckled. "Don't you worry about me, son. We'll get this all straightened out. We've got some good, smart lawyers."

That was the essence of Cloyce Box: always at his best in a crisis. He just sat at his desk, completely unflappable, quietly studying the trial transcript as if someone had just handed him a new best seller that he was anxious to get into. It wasn't a matter of false bravado or machismo. Nor was it purely ego. My father was simply a fearless man—too fearless, in fact. It was the thing that made him great.

Looking back now, I realize it was also what destroyed him.

*W*ith some reassurance that Dad was okay, I strolled over to Tom's office, which was just around the corner from Dad's office. We were soon joined by Don. I don't remember where Gary was, but he didn't join us that evening. It was just the three of us, sitting there and bemoaning the horrible ruling. Tommy gave us a detailed account of the proceedings. He answered all of our questions. Then he grew quiet. I was right; the trial had been hard on him.

That evening in Tom's office, there was a subtle shift in our family's enterprise. All of a sudden, the patriarch didn't seem so invincible anymore. In less than a year, we knew, he would turn seventy. Dad had already gifted most of the ownership to us. It was time for the Box brothers to step up.

I uncharacteristically took the lead in the conversation. "You know, there's a lot of stuff about this lawsuit I don't understand," I began, "but there's one thing I know for sure—we've got to settle this thing. We can't go on fighting forever. We can't afford to be messing around."

"No one's been messing around—I guarantee you that," Tom shot back quickly.

I ignored his rebuke. "This Simplot guy has all the money in the world. He can spend a lot more money on lawyers than we can. We can't do this forever. If we don't settle this thing *now*, I'm afraid we never will."

Don crossed one heavy leg over the other and chimed in. "Oh, I think that's absolutely right, lad. You hang around the courthouse long enough, sooner or later someone's gonna hand your dick to ya."

With that, he folded his hands behind his head, leaned back on the couch, and gave a smirky grin. Don was saying all the right things, but his body language was telling me something different. I had my suspicion that a part of him was pleased with the ruling; it served to validate some of the things he'd been saying for years. Now perhaps someone would start to listen to him.

Ignoring Don for the moment, I looked over at Tom and said, "Okay, so where do we go from here?"

"We have to appeal," Tom replied.

"Really? There's no way we can settle?"

"Nope. We just have to beat him."

Chapter 22

BLEAK HOUSE

Leading up to the trial with Simplot, Dad had been willing to let his attorneys do most of his talking. After the trial, however, things changed. Dad was now willing to give Mr. Simplot his undivided attention, and thus the dynamics between the two of them changed dramatically. From early December of 1992 to the end of June 1993, the two men worked hard to hammer out an agreement to settle the case.

With the attorneys out of the way, they were able to make tremendous progress.

And yet a number of factors made the suit virtually impossible to settle. The first issue was Mr. Simplot's age. The lawsuit was difficult for even the experts to understand, and the eighty-six-year-old billionaire had trouble appreciating the nuances involved in settling such a complicated case.

Dad's age was also a factor. He was sixty-nine. He had heart problems and chronic high blood pressure. A year or two earlier, he'd also been diagnosed with Parkinson's disease. Dad was in poor shape physically to take on such a draining task—not to mention the challenges created by the recent bankruptcy of the cement company.

The biggest obstacle, however, was Mr. Simplot's insistence that the board of Box Energy "roll her back to a co-op." This was a term he borrowed from the farm industry, and he was using it to suggest that the board should convert Box Energy from a C corporation back into a master limited partnership. Dad knew the board would never go for that.

"I'll take it to the board; I hope it works," Dad replied over and over to Mr. Simplot's demands that he "roll her back to a co-op." "There's nothing I'd like to see more than J. R. Simplot off of my ass. Hope you're not offended."

"There's only one way you're going to get me off, Box," Simplot retorted. "Go tell your board what I want, and try to get it for me. If you don't want to try, then forget it."

"All right," Dad agreed. "I'll get the lawyers to put something together. You can always give me heck. You've given me enough trouble for a lifetime."

"Fella, you've given us trouble too, and don't you forget it," Mr. Simplot snapped back.

Of course, the real crux of the lawsuit was control of the pipeline. Mr. Simplot wanted the pipeline returned to the company, and he wanted Dad to pay $8 million in damages for having "taken" it. Dad was certain that the board wouldn't go for that either. There were potential environmental risks with owning the pipeline that made it more advantageous to keep it off of the company's books. Of course, Dad also had personal money tied up in it, so he wasn't eager to make that concession either. Complicating all of this were many other issues that involved Dad's control of the board of directors through his voting shares and the question of whether the jury's verdict required Dad to give up the pipeline, or whether it simply required him to pay damages for it.

Another compounding problem was the enormous amount of attorney's fees. The case had been allowed to drag on for so long that the fees on both sides had mushroomed into the millions.

Dad went out of his way to treat Mr. Simplot firmly but cour-
teously. On numerous occasions, Mr. Simplot made inflammatory
remarks that might have led a lesser man to lose his cool. But not
Cloyce Box. He never once went for the bait. He wasn't the least bit
afraid of escalating the dialogue whenever it might be helpful to his
cause, but he never once let his emotions get the best of him in what
had to be the most difficult negotiation of his life. It was a gift he had.
He was more than a good negotiator; he was a master at it, and never
was it on better display than during these testy negotiations.

Hindsight is always 20/20, but I believe that if the two men could
have met face-to-face, rather than talking by phone, the case could
have—and should have—been settled. An experienced mediator
could have helped as well. It boggles my mind to contemplate what
these two captains of industry might have accomplished if they could
have ever worked together as partners instead of adversaries.

Deep down, I think the two men liked each other. I know they
respected one another.

True to form, by the end of these talks, Dad was able to convert his
perennial foe into an ally. Once deeply divided, the two men became
friendly, and I don't believe that the courteous banter they began to
engage in was completely contrived.

In the end, Dad was able to convince Mr. Simplot to give up on
bringing the pipeline back to the company. This was nothing short
of a phenomenal breakthrough, considering the jury's original findings. In addition, even though the idea of "rolling her back to a
co-op" proved implausible, Dad was able to persuade Mr. Simplot
into taking his proportionate share of the company and converting it
into a limited partnership that he could control independently of Box
Energy. Mr. Simplot didn't just like this idea; he loved it.

Tragically, the agreement they came to in principle could never be
realized in practice. The derivative case was simply too complex, with

too many competing interests involved to ever be finalized. Above all, the lawyers on both sides stood to gain too much by keeping the case alive rather than by letting it die through settlement.

"My lawyer won't let me do anything but go back to the judge," Mr. Simplot told Dad. "He says that if I settle with you, they say I'll absolutely get sued by every stockholder in the country. He says that I won the lawsuit, and that this is a joint lawsuit." Mr. Simplot paused. "Anyway, he's my attorney, and I reckon that stands. I told you that I'd do anything that I could, but . . . he just won't let me do it, Cloyce."

"I thought we had a deal," Dad replied dolefully.

In spite of Dad's remarkable performance, the settlement wasn't meant to be at that time—and sooner than anyone expected, Dad's time would run out.

Chapter 23
FAREWELL TO A KING

My father celebrated his seventieth birthday in 1993. In spite of reaching this milestone and all of the stress of the last seven years, he continued to work full time, and he flew his King Air on almost a daily basis. But Dad was not well.

After discovering a heart condition in his earlier years, Dad began making semiannual treks to Duke University's renowned cardiology program located in Durham, North Carolina. He became obsessed with his health, gave up alcohol completely, and religiously stuck to a diet of lean poultry or fish, white rice, and fruit. Here was a man who could eat like a king, and yet he'd subsisted on these bland staples for the last ten years of his life.

In late October 1993, Dad was scheduled for another physical examination at Duke. I called him at the ranch early on the morning of his departure. Since his diagnosis of Parkinson's, I'd tried to keep a closer eye on him.

"My stomach's upset today," he told me. I think it was the first time in his life I'd ever heard him complain about how he felt.

*D*ad piloted his King Air up to Durham, North Carolina. Accompanying him on the trip was his wife, Ashley, his brother Boyce, and Arthur Mitchell, his chief counsel and an old friend who'd attended law school with him many years before.

They ate a spartan meal for dinner and spent the night in a nearby hotel. Early the next morning, they would check into Duke to begin their physicals.

Shortly after midnight, Ashley rolled over in bed, disturbed. Dad was still. Too still. Ashley held her breath, but she still couldn't hear a thing. She sat up in bed, peering through the darkness.

"Cloyce?" she whispered as she reached over and touched him gently. Dad was a light sleeper, but he gave no response. Ashley shook him a little harder. She repeated his name. Nothing.

She grappled for the switch and turned on the bedside lamp. Finally, she confirmed what she'd already feared: sometime in the night, Dad had suffered a heart attack. He was gone.

I was out of town when I received a call the next morning around eleven a.m.

"Douglas, is that you?" It was Dad's secretary, Kathy. "Hold on for Tommy, he needs to speak to you right away."

When Tom came on the line, I could tell I was on a speakerphone. I could hear the muffled voices of Don and Gary in the background.

"Hey Doug, did you hear about Dad?" Tom asked.

"No."

"He flew up to North Carolina," Tom said evenly. "He died."

Shock raced through my body. I couldn't speak for several moments. In a shaky voice, I managed to ask, "How did he die?"

"He had a heart attack in his sleep," Tom said. "He went to sleep and didn't wake up."

I couldn't say anything. Eventually Don spoke into the awkward silence.

"Yeah, it was a totally fucked-up deal, lad. You know, Dad had that funny heart problem. It was just one of those deals where things just didn't go right, and next thing you know—POW—it's all over."

"Hey Douglas, this is your brother Gary. Yeah, it's pretty sad around here. Everybody's pretty fucked up about CK. I don't think he even knew that he was dying, or that he was going to die." Gary struggled to find his words. "Pretty good way to go, if you ask me, and at least Ashley was with him."

I appreciated Gary trying to comfort me. I fought to maintain a false bravado; I didn't want my brothers to see me as weak.

"I guess I need to come home then," I said, "but I might stay up here one more night just to let things sink in before I drive back home and face hell."

"It's going to be hell, all right," Tom agreed. "Drive safe on your way back, now," he added.

My first phone call after I hung up was to my mother, who had already heard the news. As soon as her voice came on the line, I bawled like a baby. She was still the only person I could trust with anything.

I spent one more night in Hot Springs. None of us had expected our father to die so young. He'd always seemed so invincible that we were sure he'd live well into his nineties. I'd spoken to him just yesterday, and now he was gone, just like that.

I thought about the business as well; it was impossible not to. My brothers and I all believed that the stress of the litigation had contributed to his heart failure. I didn't think about what lay in store for me and my brothers. It wasn't the time to think about that just yet.

At eight p.m., I turned on *Monday Night Football*. During a replay, Frank Gifford announced Dad's death on national TV. I was so moved by that, and I can still remember the condolences he sent out to Ashley and to the four of us boys.

*W*hen I returned to Dallas the next day, I headed straight for Dad's office. If he's still alive, I thought, he'll be sitting at his desk, just like he was after the trial with Simplot. If he's not there, I'll know for sure that he's really gone.

After the five-hour drive from Hot Springs to Dallas, I walked into Dad's office. I found Tom standing behind Dad's desk. He was holding a drawer upside down over a trash can and giving it a few light taps to loosen the debris inside. Cardboard boxes sat stuffed with memorabilia and family portraits. Dad had a lot of framed pictures of family, including his four grandchildren, scattered around the nooks and crannies of his office. Most of them were wrapped up in newspapers now, packed away for storage.

"How was your drive?" Tom asked as soon as he saw me.

"Fine," I said. "Wow, it looks like you're moving in."

"Yeah, I need to get all my stuff in here. I can't work in here with all these pictures on the walls." Tom shot me a measured look. "I hope that doesn't bother you. Does that bother you?"

"No." I chuckled lightly. "I mean, it's a little abrupt. But Dad's gone—somebody needs to use his office."

"All right," Tom said. Then he went back to his work. I turned and walked out.

I'd meant what I said to him. Tom had a lot of things on his mind and a company to run. I was relieved that someone was ready, willing, and able to take control. I had a lot of faith in him. But I do remember thinking: Wow, that was fast. Maybe a little *too* fast.

*T*wo days later, my brothers and I gathered at the Lovers Lane United Methodist Church in Dallas for our father's memorial service. He had been our hero, our savior, and at times our adversary. Much like his life, my father's send-off was an over-the-top affair. The nine-hundred-seat main sanctuary was packed with mourners, and the outpouring of grief and support from what seemed like thousands of friends and visitors was overwhelming.

My father's memorial service wasn't the largest I've ever attended, but the service Ashley put together was a perfect tribute and reflection of his life. Frank and Kathie Lee Gifford flew in from New York. Frank gave the main eulogy and told the kind of old football stories that only someone of his stature could pull off.

"I first met Cloyce Box at the 1952 Pro Bowl Game," Frank began. "He was the most dangerous deep threat in the league. I played defense at that time, and I was supposed to cover him. Well, I couldn't cover him with a blanket. I needed a gun. No one could ever cover him man to man. He was too fast. He wasn't the greatest athlete I ever saw, but he was so darn fast, he blew by me like I was standing still."

Kathie Lee sang "He Giveth Me Grace." Dad's old friend John Wood, former head pastor at the First Baptist Church in Waco, gave several Old Testament lessons. Ashley's close friend Dianne Cash soloed on "Amazing Grace." Amazing, indeed. No one in attendance came away unmoved.

Halfway through the service I spotted Ruth Ann, my soon-to-be ex-wife. We didn't attend the memorial together that day, nor was she seated with my family, but I was surprised and touched when I looked up and saw big tears streaming down her face. Even though she and Dad got off to a rocky start, he eventually won her over, just like he did everyone else.

Seated down near the front and off to the side of the main sanctuary was Dad's youngest sister, my Aunt Tom. She and Dad had always been close, and his sudden death was a severe blow to her. Cloyce was more than just Aunt Tom's big brother; she'd looked up to him with the same adoration a child has for a father.

Aunt Tom had a good view of the many people who came to pay their last respects, and she surveyed the mourners as they filed in from all directions. Most of those in attendance, she noticed, were exceedingly well-dressed men. *Now that's odd*, she thought. *Why so few women and so many men?*

She leaned over to her son, who was seated next to her, and whispered: "Lee, I can't believe how many men are here. I've never seen so many men at any funeral before in my life!"

Lee looked around and nodded in agreement, but Aunt Tom wasn't satisfied. She leaned in again and whispered more firmly, "Men don't usually go to funerals, you know. Do you know who all these men are?"

Lee nodded again. This time he leaned in close to his mother's ear so as not to be heard.

"Yeah, I do, Mom," he said. "They're lawyers."

PART II

The Fall of a Family Business

"We have met the enemy . . . and he is us."

—From "Pogo" by Walt Kelly

Chapter 24

SUDDEN DEATH

Death has a way of uniting families. When Dad passed away, my three brothers and I were all naturally drawn together by our mutual loss. Throughout the flourish of mourning activity, everyone was on their best behavior.

The timing of Dad's death in late October may have contributed to our sense of solidarity, as the holidays would soon be upon us. A week after the memorial service, Aunt Tom and her daughter Lanie drove over from Fort Worth. It was the first holiday season after Dad's death, and Aunt Tom did a lot of reminiscing.

"I was thinking of a Christmas we had with Cloyce and Fern when y'all lived on Park Lane," she recalled. "I remember making a Pillsbury Cook-Off winner called Dilly-Cheese Bread, cooked in a tube pan. I took it to their house.

"A colored man—an employee, I believe—called Cloyce on the phone Christmas morning. He needed someone to post his bond. When your dad asked why he was in jail, he said, 'I hit a man over the head with an RC Cola bottle.'" Aunt Tom shook her head, smiling. "We had a chuckle about that! Cloyce got him out of jail. I can't believe how many people he helped out." Her voice broke, and tears gleamed in her eyes at the memory of her brother's generosity.

Barely fifty years old, Ashley was suddenly a widow. She had adored my father, to whom she'd been married just six and a half years. After the funeral, I began to see less and less of her, and within a year or two, she had remarried another successful businessman and spent much of her time with him. Over the course of the next fifteen years, I rarely saw her. I was sad when she drifted away; she was all I had left of Dad.

Though I was deeply shocked at the loss of my father, there was another part of me that was ready—if not willing—to let him go. The therapy I'd done years before had paid off. I'd made my peace with him. While in some ways this made the loss even harder, it also gave me a sense of closure. I was grateful for that. Nothing can ever completely take away the sting of death, and yet I'd learned that there is a big difference between sorrow and regret. I had none of the latter.

But I wasn't so sure that my three older brothers could say the same. Even though he was no longer around, Dad still occupied a large place in all our lives. He especially occupied a large place in Tom's life because he and Dad had worked more closely together than the rest of us combined.

I wasn't worried about Gary or Tom. They each had a different mentality, but neither Gary nor Tom were the kind of guys to wear their emotions on their sleeves. But Don and I were the more sensitive types.

While I had great admiration for Don's intellect, I had doubts about my oldest brother's emotional well-being. Outwardly, Don's personality was playful, sometimes even cheerfully optimistic. From watching him grow up, however, I knew that he harbored a lot of bitterness. I wasn't sure what his discontent was all about, but I suspected that some of it, at least, had to do with Dad.

*P*rior to his death, Dad had done quite a bit of estate planning. He'd of course transferred the equity shares in the family holding company to the four of us boys. But he'd never put together much of a succession plan. Had he stepped down well before his death, we would have had a much better chance of keeping our family and our business intact. But how do you say to the patriarch who beat the odds and created all the wealth: "Enough already. Your job here is done. Go off and play bridge!" Dad was a workaholic. Suggesting that he needed to slow down or stop working would have been like telling a smoker to quit cold turkey.

None of us had ever seriously considered that our father would die at the relatively young age of seventy. We were a bit young, too: Don, the oldest, was only forty-three, Gary was forty-one, and Tom was just thirty-eight. I was thirty-six. We were all years away from our business prime. More importantly, none of us had any real experience outside the confines of the family office. Now here we were with a massive business enterprise in a total mess, the founder permanently departed, and no sense of a common vision or clearly defined leader to follow.

Within days after the memorial service, the directors of Box Energy called an emergency board meeting. The nine-member group unanimously named Tom the new CEO. In an effort to be sensitive to family dynamics, they also offered the position of chairmanship to Don. He initially turned down the offer, but then he changed his mind a week or two later and accepted it.

Despite the fact that tradition called for the oldest male to step into the patriarch's shoes, Tom's ascension was fully anticipated. Don was on the board but had other interests, Gary certainly wasn't a candidate, and as the youngest brother, I wasn't even on the radar.

Even though I was never a director of Box Energy, I attended a number of board meetings as a guest. I remember the first one that Don ever chaired after Dad died. Don opened the meeting with a prayer. I think he learned this at St. Mark's, where chapel services were held every Wednesday morning before classes. His leadership impressed me that day, and I still think things might have turned out differently if we could have clung to some of his initial reverence.

But we were a business family. If we had any faith at all, it was in money.

Almost all of the trappings of my father's tangible power—his titles, his salary, his office—passed to Tommy instead of Don. The only thing not fully under Tom's control was our father's estate. In his will, Dad named Tom and Don as co-executors. The rationale for having two executors was simply due to the sheer size of the assets owned by my father at the time of his death.

Tom relished the opportunity to step into his father's shoes. He was so anxious to get started that he couldn't wait for his father to be buried before moving into his office. There were those who said that he almost looked euphoric after taking over his father's job, but I knew better than that. Beneath his energetic exterior, he was deeply aggrieved. It's just that he had a different way of dealing with it. Like Dad, Tom wasn't fond of looking back.

I had a lot of confidence in Tom's ability. Though young for a CEO, he possessed just about every trait a founder could ever want in a successor. He was focused, determined, organized, and tough-minded. It's true that he may not have had quite the IQ that our scholarly brother had, but he sure made up for it in more important ways, including his ability to connect with people. Tom was also a strong-willed guy, and whatever he set his mind to, he could do pretty darn well. When it came to leadership qualities, he wasn't just ahead of Don; he ran circles around him. For that matter, he ran circles around me as well. To cap it all off, his law school background was the perfect fit for the jumble of lawsuits we were in.

I had little doubt that he could run the company and simultaneously contend with the mountain of litigation. What I wasn't so sure about was how well he could lead the *family*. Though similar to Dad in temperament, Tom was still our brother, not our parent, and he could ill afford to lead the family the same way our father had.

My brothers and I were all undergoing tremendous upheaval. The enterprise was in litigation free fall, and our father's estate was bankrupt. The board might have named Tom the leader of the business, but no board could name him leader of the family; that had to come from within. If we were going to make it through this dark night, one of us would have to emerge as the leader, and soon.

*T*om first met his wife while they were both in law school at Baylor University. After finishing college in 1983, they continued to date for several more years, but they didn't marry immediately. Tom promptly moved back to Dallas to work in the family office, while his wife moved back to the small town in East Texas where she'd grown up. It was there that she took over her father's lucrative law practice and ran for county judge as a Democrat. Eventually, she won a seat on the bench and became the local judge.

Over the course of the next five years, both of them became deeply entrenched in their respective and promising careers. Tom resided in Dallas, while she lived a two-and-a-half hour drive away in East Texas. Their long-distance relationship meant that they spent a lot of time driving back and forth over the weekends, holidays, or other special occasions.

Finally, in 1988, they decided to marry. But after the wedding, they continued to live apart. Even when their only son was born in 1992, they maintained separate residences.

To compensate, Tom spent an increasing amount of time in East Texas in the years leading up to Dad's death. Even when he was with us in Dallas, we all knew his time was fleeting. He was trying to be in two places at one time. It put a strain on him that everyone could feel, and over time, his continued absence extracted a toll on the bonds of our sibling partnership. Ever so slowly, the natural born leader of the family grew further and further apart from his brothers.

And then, when Tom became CEO, his workload exploded. With virtually no time to spend with us during weekends or holidays (and perhaps even less so with his family in East Texas), communication between the four brothers began to grind to a halt at the worst possible time.

Trust wouldn't be far behind.

Chapter 25

A BIG STICK

Toward the end of Dad's life, he was paid an annual salary of $1,000,000. Along with the income from the pipeline, this salary had been keeping his vast empire afloat: the private-side payroll, the expense of running three big ranches, alimony payments to my mother, and a backlog of other debts and obligations.

But a dead man can't earn a salary, and soon Dad's estate defaulted on most of its obligations. It wasn't long before our accountants dourly reported that his estate had a negative net worth of some $80 million. This was a blessing in disguise, as neither Simplot nor any other creditor could collect against an insolvent estate.

The big house in Frisco, once the nucleus for family gatherings, had burned to the ground six years earlier. Despite his vow to rebuild, Dad was never able to do so, and after erecting the steel frame, the reconstruction project had to be halted. Dad's massive investment in the cement plant and the Ocala horse farm had drained him of cash to rebuild. My parents' divorce hadn't helped much, either. All that remained of the house once known as the original Southfork was a skeletal structure that stood in effigy of a once proud Texas family.

In November 1993, our entire management team began having a series of tense meetings in the boardroom. We needed a plan to deal with the perfect storm we were caught up in. Our biggest concern had to do with Simplot's takeover efforts. What would happen, we wondered, if the court entered a final judgment against us? We didn't want to wait around and find out.

After hours of sometimes-heated debate, we decided that BBHC needed to hire a law firm to represent its interests against my father's estate. Tom and Don had already hired a law firm of their own choosing to represent them as co-executors. Since they were "conflicted out" from acting on behalf of BBHC, and since Gary wasn't that keen on attending to such matters, the job of finding a good lawyer fell to me.

A couple of years earlier, I'd made a casual acquaintance of an attorney named Rockney D. "Rock" Pletcher. Rock was the younger brother of Dad's longtime thoroughbred horse trainer, Jay J. Pletcher, and he was a board-certified estate lawyer with one of the big law firms in downtown Dallas. He was also a CPA. Because of their longtime association with my family, I had always liked and trusted the Pletchers.

A few weeks before Christmas of 1993, I drove down to Rock's office, where we sat and talked for hours. This was the first of many meetings. He helped me understand the situation we were in, and he convinced me that we needed to take an aggressive stance against the creditors of Dad's estate. Rock spoke like a disarming ol' country boy, a quality he used to his advantage against opponents, who failed to notice that under the "dumb hick" exterior, he was smart as a whip. During that conversation, he reminded me very much of my maternal grandfather, and I instantly took a liking to him. Soon after, I agreed to hire him on behalf of BBHC.

During one of our strategy sessions, we collectively stumbled upon a fortuitous discovery. During his lifetime, Dad had borrowed millions from BBHC, the family holding company that my brothers and I now owned. Prior to his death, he'd pledged all of his stock in Box Energy as collateral against his debt to us. Part of that pledge required him to make interest payments on the debt, but soon after he died, his estate defaulted on the payments. This "event of default" gave BBHC the right to foreclose on a big block of Box Energy stock, valued between $20 and $30 million, that Dad owned at the time of his death. This was the same block of stock that Simplot was trying to get by suing us.

As soon as Rock heard about this, he became an ardent proponent of foreclosing on this stock in order to get it out of Dad's bankrupt estate. He thus became the chief architect of the deal that became infamously known as the "February Transaction."

There was no sense in denying it: the February Transaction would be a risky proposition. If we wanted to save the family enterprise, we knew we had to do something. But in order for the February Transaction to succeed, we needed to get all of the thorny details just right; if someone made a careless mistake, the entire transaction could be overturned. Apart from that, we knew full well that even if we succeeded, Simplot would sue us again. And Simplot wasn't our only problem; we had other creditors as well. Did it make sense to give them another cause of action? What other options did we have? What if we did nothing?

I ruminated in this fashion over whether or not we should pull the trigger. Rock would argue in favor of the deal by telling me: "Doug, ya gotta get a big stick."

Aside from that, we were Cloyce Box's sons. We couldn't help but have some of his maverick business sensibility in our genes. So even with all of the potential dangers in mind, we decided to move forward.

*F*rom the end of January through most of February of 1994, Tom and I worked feverishly alongside a small army of lawyers on both sides to complete this emotionally draining transaction. A series of terse negotiations took place between the various lawyers in the deal, followed by terse meetings between Tom and me. This block of stock represented the estate's biggest asset, and Tom was leery of removing it. What's more, Tom, a pugnacious guy by nature, didn't like Rock, and seemed to be enjoying me less and less by the day.

For my part, I wasn't too happy with Tom, either. He and Mr. Simplot had begun sparring with each other almost immediately after Dad's death, spoiling some of the goodwill that Dad had achieved, and I was disappointed that Tom wasn't doing more to encourage a settlement. I had tried to warn him to do so right after the jury trial, while Dad was still alive, but Tom said that we had to appeal. He seemed to enjoy the thrill of corporate warfare a bit too much for my taste. I certainly admired his determination, but I didn't always respect his contentious approach to things. Right or wrong, I held Tom accountable for some of the mess we were in.

One day while the two of us were meeting in what I still thought of as Dad's office, I found him in a foul mood. It was a look I recognized from childhood.

"What's wrong?" I asked. "What are you so pissed off about?"

"What am I pissed off about?" He began ratcheting himself up. "You want to know what I'm pissed off about?"

"Yeah."

"I'm pissed off at you, that's what!" Tom glared at me.

"What for?"

"Because you ask the dumbest questions." He seemed to be getting angrier by the word.

"I don't ask dumb questions," I said.

"Yeah, I'm afraid you do. You ask so many dumb questions. It used to make Dad mad, you know."

By saying that, he was playing on some of my deepest insecurities, and he knew it. But I was known to have a temper as well.

"There's no such thing as a dumb question, if you ask me," I shot back.

"No one asked you. And no one around here cares what you think. Everyone here thinks you're a dumbass. Did you know that?"

His words cut hard at me. I was angry and hurt, but not too hurt to talk back. My emotions flared out of control, and my mouth wasn't far behind. I don't remember what I said, but we yelled and cussed and called each other crazy. Our shouting match went on for so long and grew so loud that we cleared out the secretarial pool that sat right outside Dad's office. I finally picked up the thick set of documents I'd brought to discuss with him, tossed them across the table like they were a weapon, and got up and stormed out.

If Dad had been around, nothing like this would have been possible. Instead, Tom and I were left to run amok. Compounding the problem was the fact that each of us had our own set of attorneys, who I think were subconsciously (or maybe consciously) trying their best to pull us apart.

While I might have been too intimidated to ever openly confront my father, I wasn't the least bit afraid of my brother. Nor was he the least bit afraid of me. So right then and there, I made up my mind: if my brother wanted a fight, I was ready to give him one.

Chapter 26

RACING TOWARD DISASTER

As Tom and I grappled with each other over the terms and conditions of the February Transaction, Don had a dramatically different perspective on the adversity we faced. In a way, he may have seen it as an opportunity to make a substantial contribution to the family business at last.

During the early 1990s, Don's disillusionment with the business had reached a pinnacle. Sandwiched as he was between two charismatic men—his iconic father on the one hand and his younger, more dashing brother on the other—Don had felt superfluous for many years. No one seemed interested in listening to anything the director of corporate development had to say, and even though Don remained a fully salaried employee, he had long since given up on making any significant contribution to the organization.

His response to the noisy forces threatening to take the family enterprise asunder was to simply write it all off. This did not mean, however, that he was totally passive. Five years earlier, Don had begun working diligently but quietly, behind the scenes, to take the family in a completely new direction.

As a youngster, his biggest hobby had been fine cars and professional motor sports. He owned go-karts as a kid that he raced at amateur tracks around the Dallas/Fort Worth metroplex. He read magazines like *Motor Trend* and *Car and Driver* from cover to cover, and he owned a Shelby GT 500 that he only got to drive for a couple of years before it was stolen during his freshman year at Penn. Still, the muscle car reinforced his passion for sports cars and auto racing.

Once or twice a year, Dad flew him up to watch the big races. They even went to the Indy 500 a couple of times. In his thirties, when he had little more to do than clock in and out of the office, he briefly resurrected his go-kart racing hobby.

After my parents divorced in 1986, Mom acquired a good bit of wealth. She knew little about managing money, so she asked Don to do it for her. He leaped at the chance, relishing the opportunity to prove himself to his mother, since he couldn't seem to do so with his father. Don became Mom's trusted financial advisor, helping her put in place all kinds of things like life insurance, investments, and various trust agreements.

Don did a fine job, and after a year or so had gone by, Mom's finances were well in order. Under her generous settlement agreement with Dad, she soon had more money than she would ever know what to do with. She had happily remarried an air force veteran who treated her like royalty. She and her new husband lived a quiet but active life that she spent attending church, singing in the choir, traveling, and of course enjoying her grandchildren.

Although things were working out wonderfully for Mom, Don now found himself out of a job and somewhat despondent. With nothing to do at the office all day, he took to driving over to her house, where he bellyached relentlessly about the gloomy outlook for the family enterprise. He certainly had a point: the family *was* facing a crisis. But rather than working to confront these challenges head on, Don preferred to rant to his mother about his exaggerated version of hopelessness and despair. He spent hours pacing around the freshly painted millwork and marbled flooring of her three-story home like some filibustering senator pouring out objections to a hotly contested bill.

One day, he came up with what he thought was the perfect solution to everyone's problems, and he went to see his mother with a different agenda in mind.

He began by painting such a grim picture of the family business that even Mom had to agree it was the worst situation anyone could ever imagine. "The oil business is doomed, Mom, and we have *no* chance whatsoever to survive. But my buddies and I, we're some of the smartest guys out there. We've done *all* the research." Mom sat in silence, unsure of how to respond, listening to him. "We can show you beyond a shadow of a doubt exactly how and when Box Energy is going belly-up. But we've also figured out a plan."

He went on to explain at length that Dallas–Fort Worth was one of the few major markets left in the country without a "Division 1" auto raceway. His idea was to finance and build a NASCAR-style racetrack here in the Dallas area. Similar in nature to the cement plant, this would be a "greenfield" project, meaning that Don would have to acquire the land, raise the capital, design the track, and then carefully construct the raceway according to NASCAR's specifications. His business school buddies helped convince Mom that they had done a thorough investigation of the viability of the raceway and that it would be a major source of income for years to come.

In order to kick-start the project, he needed Mom to hand over a million bucks of her own money. These funds would be used for working capital and developmental expenses.

Don explained how the racing business would not only provide all four of us brothers with a job for the rest of our lives, but that it would also provide a better complement than the oil business for each of our skill sets. As the only real mechanic of the family, Gary would have a dream job. My interest in television and the media business would be a great fit in the marketing-dominated industry of auto racing. Tom could always find work as an attorney, and of course Don himself, as the one with the interest in racing, would be the kingpin.

Conceptually, it wasn't a bad plan. But as with any new business venture, there were major obstacles. For one, apart from his go-kart hobby, Don was a complete unknown to the big-time auto sports industry. For another—and a much bigger issue—Don had no real money and no committed investors. He was hoping that Mom would be the first, and that her money would allow him to go in search of the rest of the $30 million he needed for the project.

Mom listened intently to Don's pitch, but initially she wasn't convinced. It was plainly a risky investment, and Mom didn't like the idea of losing money, since she had no way of replacing it.

When Mother voiced her well-founded concerns about "loaning" money to Don's racetrack venture, he said: "It's okay, Mom, we don't have to do this deal. Maybe poverty won't be all that bad. But I can tell you one thing, your grandkids are going to be eating out of dumpsters!"

Mother was new to the wealth game. She didn't have anyone to warn her about the pitfalls of family money. Her one trusted advisor was Don, and he wanted her to invest in this deal. She knew he was unhappy, and she wanted to help him. In short, she had nothing but the best of intentions, but she fell into the trap that so many wealthy people fall into: throwing money at someone's problems in the hope that it will fix their life. Like our father, she enabled Don to be less than his best self.

I think, ultimately, that Don had the best of intentions. He was trying to do what he truly believed was right for our family. But in trying to do what he believed was right, he showed that he was more than willing to use fear to manipulate our mother. In the end, those tactics worked; Don and his associates finally prevailed in persuading her to "loan" them the funds Don was asking for.

The easy part—getting money from our mother—was over. The real work of getting the rest of the money from angel investors was about to begin. Despite the long odds of it, for a few years Don seemed happy and excited to be out chasing his dream of bringing the first ever Division I raceway to the Dallas–Fort Worth marketplace. It also brought Mom some needed relief as well, as she liked to think she'd done something to make him happy. (And indeed she had.)

The venture also helped to ease the pressure from the poor relationship between Dad and Don. Although Dad had strong doubts that Don could pull the racetrack idea off, he nevertheless applauded his son's entrepreneurial bent. And it certainly was a lot of fun for my oldest brother to carry on as if he were some big-time motor sports financier, wining and dining prospective investors while charging every single outing to his wealthy mother's accounts.

*D*uring the time that Tom and I were beating each other up over the February Transaction, Don refused to allow himself to get sucked up into the vortex of the family business. He had every reason to think of himself as a bona fide racetrack developer, and as far as he was concerned, the imminent implosion of the family enterprise would have to take a backseat to his racetrack aspirations.

As he once kidded me: "A big part of my job is I gotta act like a big shot. If I don't act like a big shot, no one's gonna take me seriously."

February is high season in the Caribbean, and the exquisite French island of St. Bart's was calling Don's name. He chose to answer the call and scheduled a two-week vacation out of the country with his wife. Taken out of context, my oldest brother's decision to leave town on such a long trip during an unprecedented time of turmoil for the family business might at first seem frivolous and irresponsible. But in the broader context of his relationship to the racetrack business, it's a little easier to comprehend.

Whatever the context, however, the facts were these. On February 5, 1994, Don and Terri were on their way to the airport to catch their flight to St. Bart's. Before they could get out of town, Don needed to stop by the office. While he was there, one of Tom's associates brought down a stack of papers requiring his signature. Don hastily scribbled his initials right up next to Tom's on several transmittals that required his approval.

Included in the thick stack of papers was a partially filled-out stock certificate for one share of class "A" voting stock. The certificate was made out to Tom as the trustee. It had two signature lines, one of which had already been signed by my next to youngest brother. The other signature line awaited our oldest brother's John Hancock.

Tom's associate explained to Don that the stock certificate represented one new share of class "A" voting stock in BBHC. That one share would give Tom the authority to vote the shares of the holding company, as well as Box Energy. It was urgent, the associate said, that Don sign it in the event that something went wrong while Don was out of the country. "With Simplot out there, you never know," she said. If Don didn't sign the certificate, who knew? He might have to interrupt his vacation and fly home.

Don's mind was already long gone, imagining the white sand beaches and turquoise surf of the Caribbean paradise. I imagine him relishing thoughts of the champagne and pâté he might enjoy later on that evening. He gave the stock certificate a cursory glance, and then he scribbled his name across the allotted line.

He left for his trip without telling me what he'd done.

A week or so later, Don called into the office one morning from somewhere near St. Bart's. The call came in from a satellite phone. He and I spoke at length. I updated him on everything that was going on, particularly regarding our progress on the February Transaction. After we finished chatting, he asked to be transferred to Tom's office. The transfer was made, and he and Tom had a long discussion to which I was not privy. Twenty minutes later, Don's phone call was transferred back down to me, and we talked for several more minutes. I wanted to wrap up our conversation because I knew this had to be an expensive phone call.

"Don, that's about it, that's all I know," I said. "The only other thing that could be relevant is the voting stock, the class 'A' shares. According to the will, Tom gets all of those once the transaction's done. If I've been told that once, I've been told that a thousand times."

"Yep, I think that's right, lad," Don said placidly.

We hung up, and I never gave the matter another thought—at least not until sometime later, when this conversation became central to the ultimate fate of our family's business.

Chapter 27

THE FEBRUARY
TRANSACTION

A week or two later I was working in my office one morning when the phone rang. It was my attorney, Rock. The February Transaction was set to close in a few days. I assumed he wanted to go over the details of the agreement one last time, but instead of talking about the February Transaction, Rock wanted to talk about something else.

"Doug, who's got the class 'A'?" he asked.

"I'm not sure what you're talking about," I said at first. But then I remembered something and rifled through a stack of papers on my desk. "Oh wait a minute, I've got a copy of it right here."

"Whose name is on it?" he asked.

"Let's see . . . it's in Tom's name as the trustee, and it has both his and Don's signatures on it," I reported.

"They got together!" Rock shot back so loudly that I jumped. "They made a deal!"

I laughed dismissively at his cynicism. "Oh no, they didn't get together. See, this is just a temporary measure, in case there's some emergency while Don's on vacation." I was repeating what Tom's management team had explained to me.

Rock's voice held a barely contained impatience. "Do you have any idea how important it is to have some agreement over how those shares are owned and voted?"

I was confused now. I had begun to see Rock as a father figure and friend as well as my legal counsel, and I didn't want to appear incompetent to him.

"Rock, we've been studying the will for months now. The will gives Tommy all the voting shares. If I've been told that once, I've been told that a million times." A petulant whine crept into my voice.

"Yer dad's will gives Tommy ten shares," Rock countered. "Ten shares that Tommy is to hold in trust for all four of you, until you decide how you want to handle the voting rights of Box Energy. Once the February Transaction goes through, those ten shares will be redeemed."

He seemed to expect me to comprehend the significance of all this. I hated to ask the next question, but I had to. "Okay, when you say the word 'redeemed,' what do you mean?"

"It means they're no good . . . no longer in effect. It means, basically, that the holding company has *no* voting stock out there—except for this one share that Tommy issued to himself."

I took a deep breath, realizing the implications of this. "Well, Rock, I'm looking at a copy of the stock certificate right here in front of me. Don's already signed it. Doesn't that make it a done deal?" I asked.

"No, it doesn't." Rock snorted dismissively. "Don's signature on that share doesn't mean a thing. You four brothers *are* the entire board of directors of the company, right?" he asked.

"Yeah," I answered.

"Well, the board is the only one who can issue stock," Rock went on. "Tommy can't just issue himself a share and have Don sign it. The board has to do that. His share isn't valid. He's a lawyer—he knows it!"

I took another deep breath. "Okay, so what do I need to do? Go up to Tommy's office and tell him he didn't do it right? Tell him he has to tear up his one share of stock that Don signed and start all over again? I don't see him doing that, Rock."

"I'm sure he won't," Rock said curtly.

"So what do we do?" I asked.

"Here's what I'm going to do." Much to my relief, he began to take control of the situation. "I'm going to draft up a one-page agreement that says that the one share of Class 'A' is actually owned by you four brothers equally instead of Tommy as the sole trustee. You'll take that to the meeting on Saturday and present it to the brothers. Tell them this is what you think is fair, *because it is fair.*" He paused. "Now, how do you think Tom will react to that?" he asked.

"Man, you don't know my brother as well as I do," I said. "Ever since the day Dad died, I've never heard anything other than what the will says. The will says that Tom gets all the voting shares."

"No, the will says he gets all *ten* of the voting shares held by Cloyce at the time of his death. Yer Dad never owned this one share. Tommy just issued it to himself, and he got Don to sign off on it. That's not fair to you, it's not fair to Don, and it's not fair to Gary."

"I don't know, Rock," I sighed. "I think we're treading on thin ice here."

"What about Don and Gary?" Rock asked. "What will they say?"

"I think everyone considers this a done deal," I said.

"Let's hope not," Rock said, and then he dropped another bomb on me. "Unfortunately I can't be there at the closing on Saturday. But I'll have two of my associates there to help you."

That was a double whammy. I hung up the phone very unhappy. I liked Rock a lot and I wanted to do what he expected of me, but I had a bad feeling things were not going to turn out well.

*T*he closing of the February Transaction took place on a Saturday morning, February 26, 1994. Between my brothers, our lawyers, and the accountants, there were about a dozen of us in the Box Energy boardroom that day. Everyone seemed to be in a foul mood, including me. Don had just returned from his two-week vacation, but he didn't seem the least bit relaxed. Instead, he was uncharacteristically sullen.

Gary looked even more uncomfortable. "Hope y'all know I ain't sittin' 'round here on my butt all day. You got something for me to sign? Tell me where to sign the som' bitch so I can get outta here."

I did my best to placate him. Gary was one of the four directors of BBHC, and we needed his signature. "Hey, don't worry, man; this won't take all day. We just need a few signatures and we'll be done."

Tom, on the other hand, said very little, letting his attorney do most of the talking, which in hindsight was probably not a good idea.

The closing took longer than I thought. The time frame didn't sit well with Gary, but he hung in there, and by eleven a.m., we were done. We transferred all of our stock in Box Energy out of my father's insolvent estate. Now the stock was owned by BBHC, against which Mr. Simplot had neither a claim nor a judgment. After spending seven years and millions of his own money to take over this tiny oil company, Mr. Simplot was now faced with the prospect of starting all over at the age of eighty-five.

Could he sue to reverse what we had just done? Of course he could. In fact, we expected him to. Like Rock said, to negotiate with Simplot, we needed a big stick. Now we had one.

There was just one thing left to take care of, I knew. Before everyone had a chance to get up and leave, I cleared my throat and tentatively addressed the room, feeling defeated before I'd even begun. The scene before me felt eerily reminiscent of the time in Oklahoma City when I'd tried to present the prenuptial to Ruth Ann. Now I was broaching the topic of another contentious matter, this time in a room full of lawyers. I didn't feel as if this exchange was going to turn out any better than the one before.

"Okay, well there's one more thing we need to take care of today." I passed out copies of Rock's one-page document to everyone. "As y'all know, there's one share of class 'A' voting stock that's been issued to Tom." No one made eye contact with me as I spoke. "This document that I'm passing out here stipulates that the one share is not owned solely by Tommy, but by the four of us brothers equally, with Tom as the trustee. I hope we can—"

Tom's estate lawyer snatched up my document and scowled at me. "And I am advising my client not to even consider such a document." He laid a solicitous hand on Tom's shoulder. "This document means absolutely nothing. It has no force or effect whatsoever."

The strength of his rebuke caught me off guard, and I wasn't sure what to say. "Well . . . I was just hoping that we could . . . have an agreement . . . about—"

"As we have discussed many, many times," he interjected, "the one share of class 'A' is owned by Thomas D. Box as the trustee, in accordance with your father's will."

No one else uttered a word, not even the two associates Rock had sent to back me up. I was hoping Don might pipe up on my behalf, but he remained mute the entire time.

"Well," I began sheepishly, "I suppose if no one's willing to discuss this, there's nothing more for us to do."

The meeting adjourned with everyone feigning an air of ease and cordiality.

*B*ecause the **February** Transaction resulted in a change of control over the ownership of a public company, Box Energy had to file certain notices with the SEC. The company also had to issue a press release. When word got out about the February Transaction, all hell broke loose.

The news may have ignited the ire of the federal judge in the Simplot suit. A month following our press release, he issued a final judgment against Dad's estate. He took the jury's original verdict of $28.5 million and amped it up to $50 million to account for prejudgment and post-judgment interest. He then effectively took the pipeline away from us by imposing a "constructive trust" over the private company that owned it, CKB Petroleum.

On a pretty Saturday morning two weeks later, a process server caught up with me out at the ranch. After cracking open the thick envelope, I soon found out that Simplot had indeed filed suit against each of the four brothers for fraud and conspiracy. He was asking for $50 million in damages. Even though we fully expected this to happen, when I saw my name listed as one of the individual defendants, it ruined a perfectly good day.

The local press even took a shine to the story. The *Dallas Observer*, an edgy, alternative weekly newspaper, ran a front cover story entitled "Fit To Be Fried." It was all about our war with the Potato King.

Chapter 28

HOUSE OF CARDS

As much trouble as the February Transaction stirred up for us in the outside world, it created even more problems on the inside.

When Dad died, he owned the controlling interest in Box Energy, which was represented by 1,870,000 shares of common stock. With a market price that fluctuated between $10–20 per share, this block of stock had a street value between $20 and $30 million (give or take). If these shares had remained within the estate, Don and Tom, as co-executors, would have had equal voting authority over them for as long as my father's estate was in probate. Given the size and legal complexity of everything, this process could have taken years to complete.

But now that BBHC owned the controlling interest of Box Energy, whoever controlled BBHC essentially controlled every-thing: both the public and the private side of our businesses. Tom's "A" share not only gave him full command of the board, it virtually nullified Don's power.

Needless to say, my oldest brother didn't like the February Trans-action. In time, he would become a much harsher critic of it. But for now, focused as he was on his racetrack, he seemed content to sit back and let Tom wrangle over what to do with Box Energy along with the Simplot imbroglio.

/n the meantime, the storm rolled on.

In July 1994, a summary judgment for $25 million was rendered against Dad's estate regarding the tract of land from the ranch that Dad had pledged as collateral for the cement plant years before. For me, the worst fallout of this judgment occurred four months later on November 1, 1994: the day the bankers who held the loan foreclosed on the biggest portion of the Frisco ranch.

I was living on a small parcel of the property that Mom still owned, thus making it immune from the Bank Group's claims. Ruth Ann and I had just gotten divorced, and I had moved out to one of the guesthouses while I got my life back together.

That morning, I watched the sun rise over the remains of the big house from my porch, feeling helpless and dejected at the loss of my childhood home. It felt as if I was losing twofold: both the new family I had tried to create with Ruth Ann and the property I had grown up on.

In November of the same year, the Crow family won a judgment of $15 million against both Dad's estate and BBHC. Two weeks later, the holding company filed for bankruptcy in Delaware.

The bankruptcy process took more than a year to complete. During the proceedings, the Crow family served as a friendly creditor and helped us develop a plan of reorganization. The Simplot Group, on the other hand, wasn't so nice, and they fought us at every turn. In their efforts to keep fighting us, however, they may have committed a tactical error by moving to reverse the February Transaction in bankruptcy court. The bankruptcy judge granted their motion for a mini-trial, but following an onerous set of proceedings, the judge promptly ruled in our favor.

Although it wasn't the final ruling on the underlying merits of the transaction, it was still a game changer. With the court's help, our "big stick" had just gotten bigger. It also sent a strong message to the Simplot Group that they were in for a real dogfight.

Our upset victory in Delaware bankruptcy court validated the work and risk we had undertaken with the February Transaction. It also justified the aggressive stance that Rock had advocated for. I was proud of that.

*S*oon came another surprise.

Not long after his setback in bankruptcy court, Mr. Simplot wrote an unsolicited letter to the board of Box Energy expressing his interest in buying control of the company. He offered not only to settle all of the litigation, but also to buy the company at a premium of twenty-eight percent over the current market price. His offer may have caught the board off guard, and they made no response.

A few weeks passed, and Mr. Simplot wrote the board a second time. He expressed frustration at the lack of response to his first letter and repeated his offer to purchase the company. Then came the holidays, and the issue lay dormant into 1995.

In March 1995, Simplot repeated his offer to purchase the company a third time. I presume that his legal counsel was as competent as ours, and they knew the same thing we did: the jury verdict was vulnerable to reversal. Simplot wanted to strike a deal with us before the Fifth Circuit reversed him once again.

The more I thought about selling out to Simplot, the more I liked the idea. I couldn't help but wonder what my life might be like if we could settle all of the lawsuits, sell the business, and get our hands on some real money. It sure seemed like a better way to go than to continue grinding it out in court every day.

Further, if we sold the business, all four of us would have a measure of financial independence. I could finally get out from under my father's world, away from the family business that I was never well suited to in the first place. With three older brothers, two of whom were better educated than me, I didn't see that I had much of a future in the business anyway. Don may not have been the most ambitious guy in the world, but he sure wasn't interested in doing anything with his life that didn't involve the family office. Gary was always going to be dependent on the family enterprise in some form or fashion. And Tom certainly wasn't going anywhere. But I had gone off to college and worked hard, too. I didn't want to spend the rest of my life at the bottom of the family food chain. The money we'd get from selling the business would help me start over again.

A number of other factors made Simplot's offer appealing. I had strong doubts that we could ever settle with him without selling control of the company. He was simply too old, too rich, and too determined to ever give up. The case had grown terribly complicated, with too many lawyers representing too many embittered parties. If we sold the business, it'd be a clean break.

Yet Tom was nothing if not our father's son, and he had no interest in conceding defeat by selling out to Simplot. Tom was dead set on rebuilding his father's legacy, and as far as he was concerned, we would just have to stand and fight Simplot until our last breath or our last dollar. Tom's plan called for us to simply sit tight and wait for the ruling from the Fifth Circuit, which he believed would go our way. But that could take years, and even if the Fifth Circuit gave us the ruling we wanted, the most likely outcome was that we'd have to retry the case all over again. I didn't see Simplot ever giving in.

With each passing day, I was growing more and more anxious. Just a few years earlier I'd been forced to watch helplessly while our mammoth investment in the cement plant disappeared. We'd lost everything Dad had invested—the plant, the money, and our ranch in Frisco—while others went on to reap huge returns. Box Energy was our last big asset, and I knew we had to salvage something. Yet none of my brothers seemed as concerned as me.

Before, I'd had no opportunity to offer any input because Dad had called all the shots. But Dad was gone now. If I didn't do something—if I didn't try to get Tom to seriously consider accepting Simplot's offer and selling the company—I knew I would have no one to blame but myself.

Unsure of exactly how to proceed, I began by writing a letter to Tom, urging him to discuss Simplot's buyout offer with us. I was still smarting from some of the sharp exchanges between us concerning the February Transaction, but I wasn't angry in the letter. I was, however, concerned that we might be letting an opportunity slip away. I was careful not to use the company's computer system to write this document, typing it out on my own personal computer. But I did make three copies and hand delivered them to Don, Gary, and Tom. Tom never responded to my letter, but he did finally shoot off an official response a week later to the board of Box Energy, indicating that BBHC was not interested in selling. Even though he was purportedly acting as a trustee on behalf of himself and his three brothers, he didn't bother to discuss this with us at all. Given his control over the one "A" share, I guess he felt he didn't have to.

The lack of communication further strained our relationship. Tom was unapologetic about it. He had already made himself clear:

Box Energy was not for sale. Not to anyone, and certainly not to a dark knight named Simplot. My strong-willed brother didn't care how much money the Idaho billionaire had; he didn't want a penny of it. What he wanted was to fight Simplot to the death in court, just like our father had.

Two months later, Simplot wrote a fourth letter to the board of Box Energy, again offering to acquire the company at a respectable premium and settle all outstanding litigation. This time, he sent copies of his proposal directly to Don, Gary, and me. His letter included the following verbiage:

> I am prepared to consider a significant increase in my offer if given access to certain information not currently in the public domain. I am prepared to enter into a confidentiality agreement with Box Energy Corporation to protect this information and to respond within one week of receipt of the requisite material as to revising my current offer . . . finally, I am also prepared to participate in a competitive sales process, if you determine that such a process is in the best interest of all shareholders. You should view this as indicative of my desire to maximize value for all shareholders . . . my offer will expire on May 16 unless I have received a favorable reply by that date.

Three weeks went by, and the offer expired. I realized then that our fate was sealed. We'd spend the rest of our lives in court like dark figures from a Charles Dickens novel, fighting a perpetual lawsuit so complex and incomprehensible that no one could even explain it.

Chapter 29
SEVERED

As the new leader of Box Energy, Tom had a bold agenda in mind. He wanted to aggressively transform the company into a serious oil and gas player, rather than the "lifestyle support system" it had morphed into toward the end of Dad's life.

As part of this objective, the board had to get serious about cleaning things up. One of the frequent and recurring complaints about Box Energy was its excessive overhead. Even by Texas oil company standards, our office space couldn't be considered anything less than opulent. We occupied the top two floors at Preston Sherry Plaza in Dallas. A lavishly adorned spiral staircase connected both floors. The company cafeteria sported a fully equipped, commercial grade kitchen with two full-time cooks. We served breakfast and lunch five days a week to sixty employees, free of charge, and a couple of original oil paintings by Charles Russell hung in our boardroom.

The board hired a management-consulting firm to perform a study of the company's operations. Included in the findings of their study was a recommendation that the company abolish the Office of Corporate Development. This was the department that Don had formed years ago at OKC, and that he'd since maneuvered onto the Box Energy payroll.

By making Don the chairman of the board of Box Energy, the company had given him an opportunity to step up and utilize his strategic management skills to help his younger brother expand the business. Instead of taking this challenge seriously, he'd remained obsessed with his racetrack project to a fault. I attended a few board meetings while Don was still acting as chair, and I recall him flippantly dismissing the company's performance as weak in an attempt to convince the board that Box Energy had no ability to replace its reserves. The oil business had no real future, he seemed to say, but even if it did, the ability of our current management team was dubious at best (a not-so-subtle swipe at Tom). The only real future for the organization, according to him, was to redeploy its income stream away from exploration and toward his racetrack project.

These performances had not impressed the board. Though small in scale by industry standards, Box Energy was an extremely viable company. Its annual revenue was $60 million and growing, and it had annual cash flows of $30 million, with another $40 million cash in the bank. Eighty percent of its revenue was derived from natural gas, which it still had the right to sell under the Contract at four times the market price.

Even before the consultant's report was completed, it had become clear to the board that Don was simply not interested in the oil and gas business and that his Office of Corporate Development was little more than a front for his racetrack ambitions. Box Energy had already been pondering an exit strategy for my brother. They knew removing Don had to be done with great caution; they had already made one mistake when they encouraged him to get involved, and they didn't want to make another.

But the consultant's report, when finished, gave them the leverage they needed, and the board voted to adopt the study's recom-
mendations. As a result, Don's employment with Box Energy was
officially terminated on January 31, 1995.

At first, he didn't seem to mind too much. In exchange for agreeing to resign from all his positions with the company, he received
a whopping cash "settlement" of $490,000, plus several pieces of
expensive artwork and furniture for a total package worth $600,000.

Ordinarily when someone receives a severance check of that size,
they pack up, turn in their keys, and vacate the premises. None of
these things happened in this case. When Don "left" Box Energy, he
didn't suffer the slightest disruption in his lifestyle, his office suite,
or his work routine. The *only* thing that changed was that one day he
was on the Box Energy payroll, and on the next he was on our family's. He kept the same office, the same desk, and the same pencil
holder he'd had before. It's possible that his salary may have been
lowered, but he had just pocketed $490,000 in cash. No one was
feeling all that sorry for him—including me.

When I first heard about the severance deal, I had two reactions.
The first had to do with the amount of money. I was happy that Don
was getting it, but wondered why it was so high. He'd only been an
officer and director for a short time. I guess the board was trying to
buy peace, but it struck me as more like a bribe than a severance.
"Here's a half million bucks for doing nothing; now go away and
leave us alone."

My other source of bewilderment was Don's belief that now that
he was off the board, Box Energy was more likely to finance his racetrack. This was remarkable to me: Simplot was suing every single
director who sat on the board of Box Energy, and after the infamous

pipeline deal, I knew there was no way that the board would ever approve of another related-party transaction with anyone whose last name was Box. I guess Don wanted to believe that his departure would make Box Energy's investment in his racetrack appear more "arm's length."

He managed to finesse his way before a regularly scheduled meeting and made his formal pitch. The board listened patiently to the racetrack presentation. Tom had to abstain from voting on the matter. In short order, the board returned with their unanimous vote against the funding. Don was crestfallen.

To add insult to injury, a year earlier, a wealthy investor named Bruton Smith had announced his plans to build the Texas Motor Speedway near Ross Perot Jr.'s Alliance Airport. For a while, Don might have believed that if Box Energy financed him, he could finish his racetrack first. But with a unanimous vote against him, even Don finally had to admit that all of his hopes and dreams for building his racetrack were vanquished.

I give Don credit: he came up with an intriguing concept and put forth a valiant good-faith effort to make it a reality. In retrospect, in light of all the turmoil swirling around the family name, it's unlikely that anyone would have had a chance to raise the capital. In the end, the funding was never achieved and the project never got underway. Every dime that Mom "invested" in the project was lost, spent on "business development" expenses, including payments to consultants, attorneys, architects, and Don's buddies, who were secretly on Mother's payroll for years.

*T*he worst fallout from this unhappy experience was that Don put the blame for what happened squarely on Tom's shoulders. Tom's control over the "A" share, Don contended, had somehow been the cause of both Don's own termination and the board's refusal to write him a blank check.

A few weeks after Don was let go, I got a phone call early one Saturday morning. Don and his wife Terri were in the car, headed up north to see me at the ranch. I immediately knew that something was wrong because they rarely ever came to see me up in Frisco. Don and Terri lived in a comfortable two-story house in University Park, and Frisco seemed a world away.

They both sounded distraught. When they arrived, Don looked like he had pulled an all-nighter. Terri's eyes were red and swollen from crying.

"Douglas, I cannot tell you how stressed out I am," she began. "I'm about to lose it right now! Do you know that Donnie's been fired? He has no job now. Do you know where Donnie can find a job?"

I looked at Terri like she was nuts. "Wait a minute, it's not like he doesn't have a job anymore," I tried to assure her. "He still has a salary from the pipeline company, just like Gary and I do."

Terri pulled her hair back with both hands, revealing a face full of worry. "But his salary comes from that pipeline, and with that judge out there, you could lose that pipeline and lose everything. That judge never liked Cloyce, and he doesn't like you boys much better. He likes Simplot better than he likes y'all. Donnie says it can happen any day now. What'll he do? What'll *you* do when you don't have a job anymore? Tommy's not going to take care of you. He's darn sure not going to take care of Donnie. He's already proven that."

Don crossed his arms over his heavy chest and stood there, blinking at me. "Yeah, lad, I'm almost forty-four years old. I'm too old to look for a job now. I don't have any idea how to find one, but I guess I'll have to, thanks to Tommy."

Terri became even more emotional. "I feel like someone's broken into my house and stolen everything I have!"

Puzzled, I looked at Don. "I thought you were in favor of the severance deal. You were telling me about it just a couple of weeks ago. You were getting all this dough and you were okay with it."

"I only agreed to that bullshit 'cause your genius brother assured me that Box Energy was going to build my racetrack," Don said, giving me a wall-eyed stare. "Then after they shit-canned my ass, Tommy made damn sure his board voted it down. It was all just a very carefully concocted scheme to trick fuck me."

A part of me genuinely felt sorry for him, but another side of me wanted to let him have it. *If you were so concerned about the "A" share, why did you sign the damn thing and then leave the country on a two-week vacation at the worst possible time in the history of the family? For years I've had to sit and listen to you bellyache about how incompetent your old man is, and how he never lets you do anything. Then, when you're given the chance to step up, what do you do? You run halfway across the globe so you can float around on some sailboat for two whole weeks!*

It might have done me some good to get some of that off my chest, but I was afraid that if I said those things, both he and Terri might have collapsed right there in front of me. For the next two hours, I felt like a suicide prevention operator, talking them off a ten-story ledge. We went and ate lunch, which helped calm them down, and then mercifully, after hours of incessant talking, they drove off of the ranch and went back home.

But my time as Don's sounding board was far from over.

Chapter 30

THE TRIANGLE

After Don's ignominious fall from grace, nothing in my family was ever the same. My oldest brother's delicate psyche seemed shattered, and I considered the possibility that he might have had a nervous breakdown.

For the next two years, the ramifications of these developments rippled throughout my family's system like aftershocks following an earthquake. Don seemed to become hell-bent on destroying the family and the company at any and all costs. The board may have thought that the large severance package would buy them peace, but the only thing Don seemed interested in now was vengeance. From this point on, I witnessed his behavior growing increasingly erratic.

He became convinced that Tom and a few of his people were spying on him. He even hired a detective to scan his office for bugging devices. No "bugs" were ever found, but this didn't stop him from believing otherwise.

"Aha," he exclaimed to me on his mobile phone one day, "I think I found the smoking gun!"

I tried to explain that the plug-in transformer that he found in the ceiling above his office was put there to power a speakerphone in the office above his, but he wouldn't have it.

Don's paranoia about whether or not Tom was spying probably stemmed from the fact that he was doing a good bit of spying of his own. He somehow got an extra set of keys to Tom's office and began going there late at night, rifling through Tom's desk, sifting through his files and handwritten notes. Every once in a while, Don would call me after a late night of skulking and boast about some purported find. "Lad, I think I just uncovered the Dead Sea Scrolls." I don't think he ever found anything worthwhile, but he seemed to relish his new role as office sleuth.

Don developed such a distrust of Tom that he eventually refused to be represented by the same law firm that represented Tom as one of the co-executors of Dad's estate. Don hired a separate law firm in Fort Worth. Don's new law firm charged my father's estate a lot of money to do little more than monitor the work that the other law firm was already being well paid to do. It added a fresh layer of expense to a process that was already terribly over-lawyered. But the absurdity of it all seemed lost on my Ivy League brother. It made him feel better, and that was all that mattered.

I felt like I was babysitting a middle-aged man. I did have empathy for him. He was completely out of place and hadn't ever figured out how to live up to all of his potential. Looking back, I realize now that I was a part of the dysfunctionality as well. By listening to Don for too long, I unwittingly served to enable him. The therapy I'd started in college had helped me a great deal. I benefited from talking things out, and as a result, I fell into the trap of thinking that if I listened to my brother long enough, he might get over some of his hurt. But it didn't work out that way; the more Don talked and the more I listened, the deeper and deeper a hole we dug for ourselves.

I should have insisted on a healthier set of boundaries between us. I should have told him to get help from a professional instead of me. That would have been the right thing to do. Don was a smart guy and a big thinker, but when his racetrack ambitions died, he became an emotional basket case. In the aftermath of his fall, my oldest brother had no one else to turn to but me. I couldn't abandon him now. Someone needed to sit and listen to his daily rant. I worried that if I didn't do this, he'd find someone else to talk to—for example, a newspaper reporter, one eager to exploit another story about the "crooked sons of Cloyce Box."

So I kept on listening, and I watched as Don became an increasingly harsh critic of our brother Tom. Don was determined to blame everything wrong with the business and the world at large on him. Most days around ten a.m., Don would come trudging down to my office, coffee mug in hand, to repeat his swan song about how poorly he'd been treated. He'd stand in the doorway, squinting hard at me through the thick lenses of his glasses until I looked up at him.

"Yeah, lad, just wanted to come down and see what you're up to," he'd begin.

"Oh, not too much," I'd say while letting my voice trail off, hoping he'd get the clue that some of us were trying to get some work done.

He'd wave a hand dismissively. "Yeah, well, what I'm really trying to figure out is what the rest of these morons are up to around here. After that 'A' share caper, I really can't trust anyone here anymore. Everyone works for Tommy."

Following this unveiled plea for sympathy, Don would settle into my office uninvited. He'd pull up a chair, tip it back on its hind legs, and prop his feet up on the edge of my desk. For the next several hours he'd remain locked in that position, bobbing back and forth indignantly while he spewed vitriolic fury, railing against the various insults and offenses he had endured. Our father had screwed everything up, he insisted, and now Tom had made it ten times worse. The oil business had no future. The racetrack had been our only hope, but now that was "shit-canned" as well.

For what seemed like years, I listened to his ruminations. I took to going into the office on Saturdays, thinking I could get more work done that way. But it didn't take long for him to catch on to my subtle trick, and he started coming in on Saturdays as well. Sometimes I would eat a very late lunch out of the office, hoping I could catch a break. But Don would follow me to lunch even if he had already eaten, just so he could continue bending my ear. He seemed like a lost puppy following me around.

Things got even weirder when Don tried to make me a stand-in for the conflict he was avoiding with Tom.

"Tommy," he started off one day, while looking at me squarely across from my desk, "I sure am glad I'm not like you." He got up from his chair and paced around the space in front of my desk. "You've done everything you can think of to entrench yourself in the management of this fucked-up little company. You tricked me into signing that piece of shit 'A' share when I was headed to St. Bart's." Anger shadowed his face like thunderclouds building in the sky. He tugged at the vest of his three-piece suit, trying in vain to cover his ample gut, emotions rolling off of him and roiling throughout the room. "Well, that kind of bullshit just ain't gonna cut it around here anymore."

He'd recapture a bit of his composure, but then he'd start again. "And let me tell ya one more thing, Tommy—"

"Don, stop it!" I shouted, standing up so that he wasn't towering over me anymore. "You're creeping me out with this shit. Why don't you just go talk to Tom instead of me?"

He lowered his gaze to the floor. "Oh I will, lad, I will," he replied.

But we both knew it was a hollow promise. Don had no intention of ever confronting Tom face-to-face. He was far too conflict avoidant to ever do that. As for Tom, he couldn't care less what Don thought. He had enough to worry about.

*T*rapped as I was between my two brothers, I had no idea what to do. Looking back now with the benefit of perfect hindsight, I know exactly what I *should* have done. I should have packed up my office, turned in my keys, and physically left the office. I was only thirty-seven; I had plenty of time to start over.

The great mistake I made was getting too involved.

It was quite simple; my father had left Don and Tom in charge of everything. He'd named them the co-executors of his estate and they were both on the board of the oil company. Dad left me in charge of nothing. The two businesses I knew best were both gone by now. Thus, there was nothing for me to do other than muck things up. By hanging around, I made things worse.

A few years earlier, in fact, I had tried to leave. I had no real career so I took a sales job at a music store. But less than a year later, the jury verdict in the Simplot case came down. Once again, I let my emotions lead me around by the nose. I returned to help circle the family wagon around yet another crisis.

All of my gut instincts in college had been spot on. In a broader sense, the great mistake of my life was not having enough faith in myself to trust my own instincts. Due to a poorly defined sense of self, I became too susceptible to the influence of others, too eager for their approval, too unwilling to take a responsible stance against the dictates of my father, too anxious to walk down whatever difficult path my own heart said was right for me.

I assumed it would be hopeless to reach out for help from brother Tom. But I knew I had to try, and that meant bringing up the issue of the contentious "A" share again. I made an appointment to see him, hoping this would elevate the importance of our meeting.

I hated to bother Tommy. He was working hard to expand the company's drilling operations into areas it had never been in before, such as South Texas, Mississippi, and Alabama. He seemed to love his job of running Box Energy. He was a fighter, and appeared to relish jostling with our adversaries on a daily basis. He was good at it, too.

I knew he didn't have much interest in meeting with me. He especially had no interest in discussing the one "A" share dispute. It didn't help that he didn't care for my lawyer, Rock Pletcher, and I suppose saw me as little more than Rock's puppet.

"Hey, man!" I tried to sound chipper as I plopped down in a chair not too close to his desk. "Thanks for taking some time out of your busy schedule," I said in a mocking way, trying to be funny, but Tommy didn't always find me amusing.

"Yeah, drilling about ten wells right now." He peered down at his work. "We've got a damn good team in place. Couple of guys came over from Hunt who I really like. A geologist and a geophysicist."

"Oh yeah? Well, that's good," I replied. "You sure I'm not bothering you right now?"

"Heck no. I mean, we're busy as all get out, but I have time." He sounded warm and friendly now. It reminded me of why people liked him so much, and it made me miss him. I wanted to somehow go back to being brothers again and forget about all this other stuff. I wished we could go arrowhead hunting together or shoot some baskets like we had when we were boys.

My nostalgia ended, though, when he asked: "So how's Don doing? How's Gary? How's that sonofabitch lawyer of yours?"

I chuckled at his reference to Rock. "Oh, I guess everybody's fine, for the most part. But, uh, there are some things I'd like to talk about." I paused. I wasn't sure how to proceed. I went on anyway. "I think it's safe to say there's some concern—some real concern over the voting shares and how they're owned and how they're voted and so forth." I couldn't soft-pedal it any more than that.

Tom's eyes narrowed but he spoke evenly. "I guess I just have to go back to Dad's will, Douglas. You have a copy of Dad's will, don't you?"

"Yeah." His question annoyed me a little. We'd been poring over legal documents for more than a year and a half.

"I know that the lawyers who work for you guys have come up with all sorts of fascinating legal theories," he said. "But it's pretty darn simple. Dad's will creates the trust. It names me as the trustee, and Don signed the stock certificate. What else is there to talk about?"

"Yeah, but the foreclosure on the Box Energy stock that we transferred out of Dad's estate—"

"Okay now, who told you to say that? Is that what Rock told you to say?" Tom liked to jab at Rock every chance he got.

"Yeah, he's the holding company's lawyer," I responded.

"No," Tom said. "Rock does *not* represent the holding company. He represents *you*."

I tried to redirect the conversation. "Listen, this thing over the voting shares, it's really more of an issue between you and Don than it is you and me," I said carefully. "All I'm asking you to do is just make sure we stay on the same page. It's not healthy for the four of us to have a problem, you know. I'm afraid if it goes unresolved much longer it will lead to bigger problems. I think we should all sit down and talk it through."

"Sure, I'll sit down and talk," Tom said. "But what is there to talk about? Even if the will wasn't clear about this, Don signed the darn certificate. Now he says he didn't mean to sign it?" Tom chortled. "That's a bunch of crap. Who signs a stock certificate and then says, 'Oh, I didn't mean to sign that'? You can't run a business that way."

I ignored his retort. "Look, I know you're busy and stuff, but I don't think you realize how unhappy Don is."

"What the heck is Don unhappy about?" he asked. "We just gave him half a million bucks. He told me just the other day he was perfectly fine with everything."

He was telling the truth. That's how Don could be sometimes—conflict avoidant to a fault. Here I was trying to go to bat for him, but Don wouldn't even stick up for himself.

"I don't want to speak for him," I replied. "But you know, he—he's unhappy with a lot of things."

Tom wheeled his desk chair around so that we were now facing each other more squarely. "Look, I know what this is all about. Some of the people you and Don like to talk to aren't that loyal to you guys. Y'all like to talk too much. Y'all talk to Rock too much. I have it from some very good sources that you guys want to sell out. The reason that I can't do anything about y'all's problems is that Dad put me in charge of this thing. He put me in charge of Box Brothers Holding Company through his will, and the board put me in charge of Box Energy. Now this is nothing against you personally, but let me just say something here: this company is not for sale."

The evenness of Tom's voice gave way to a building crescendo. "It's not for sale to anybody, and it's darn sure not for sale to Simplot. And anyone who tries to do anything with this company—I don't care if it's you or Don or Rock or even those pricks over in Fort Worth—need to know one thing—I won't be easy to deal with."

Chapter 31

THE UPRISING

One morning while I was driving to work I got a call from an old high school buddy. "Hey man, have you seen a copy of today's *Wall Street Journal*?"

"No, why?" I asked.

"You better stop and pick one up before you get to the office. I have to warn you, Doug, it's pretty bad."

I was used to seeing articles about the company and the takeover battle with Simplot, so I assumed it was just another article about the never-ending saga.

"What do you mean 'bad'?"

"Did you write a letter to Tom or something?" he asked me.

How could he know about that? I swallowed hard. "Yeah, way back in December."

"It's in the paper," he announced. "They've copied a part of your letter and put it right up next to a picture of Tom. You better go look at it before you hit the office. It reads like a tabloid piece." He chuckled.

"What do you mean?" I couldn't wait to go buy my own copy. "Read it to me right now!"

"It's called, 'A House Divided—Box Brothers Lock Horns Over Father's Legacy.'"

I pulled over to the side of the road, and he read the whole article out loud to me. Sure enough, it was my letter. Someone in our office had gotten hold of it and sent a copy to the *Journal*. It was the first time our sibling discord had become the subject of public scrutiny, bringing what should have been a private matter out into the open.

*O*n Monday, April 10, 1995, Tom and the attorneys who represented BBHC were set to fly to Wilmington, Delaware. The next day, they would attend a brief but important hearing in which BBHC would officially emerge from Chapter 11. Even though the bankruptcy in Delaware had been a big blessing in disguise, I was worried that if Tom's "A" share made it all the way through the reorganization without being challenged, it would give him one more argument in favor of its legitimacy.

This dispute over the "A" share had dragged on for more than a year with no sign of resolution. Don had been fired, a billionaire's offer declined, and Don and Tom's relationship was threatening to rip the company apart. It was getting harder and harder for me to stay trapped in the middle of a deepening conflict between my two strong-willed brothers, and listening to Don's versions of the same stories over and over again, day after day, was driving me batty. This couldn't go on forever. Something had to give.

So I made up my mind. I had to take action.

On the evening of Tuesday, April 11, I finally took matters into my own hands. I called Don and Gary first and told them what I had planned. I did not tell Tommy about it. I was done trying to be reasonable.

Once Don and Gary had agreed to my plan, with the three of us on the line, I dialed Tom's number at the magnificent Hotel DuPont in Wilmington, Delaware. At first, Tom sounded upbeat as the four of us exchanged nervous pleasantries. He might have been thankful that his three brothers were showing a bit more interest in all the work he was doing on our behalf, or he might have smelled mutiny.

Then I announced to the group that as the four directors of Box Brothers Holding Company, a quorum was present and this phone call was now deemed a telephonic board meeting.

As soon as I said that, Tom's attitude changed dramatically.

The conference call, which was recorded, was little more than one long, bitter argument. Throughout the conversation, Tom cleverly denounced our actions and consistently objected to the lack of notice for a board meeting required under Delaware law. By the end of the call, however, my plan had succeeded: all four of us claimed to own one share of class "A" stock of BBHC.

Tom stood his ground and never lost his cool. At the end of the call, Gary did his best to console him. "Hey man," he said, "I'm really sorry, you know—we didn't mean to fuck you up."

*T*he hearing set for the next morning was little more than a formality. BBHC was now officially out of bankruptcy.

After the hearing, Tom and his lawyers boarded a flight back to Dallas. The next evening, his attorneys treated him to a nice dinner at an upscale steakhouse. The lawyers were careful to invite all of us to dinner that night, but Don, Gary, and I knew better than to go anywhere near the restaurant after what we'd just put Tom through. This was supposed to be a celebratory occasion for the family—a victory party—but after the telephonic board meeting, I had a feeling that the only folks celebrating were the lawyers. In addition to the hefty fees they'd received during the yearlong process, they asked for a $50,000 bonus. The bonus was paid.

Still, I let myself celebrate a personal victory. Over the weekend, I basked in the glow of the successful resolution, as I saw it, to the dispute over the one "A" share. *It was a tough job, but somebody had to do it,* I thought with a touch of self-bravado. I waxed philosophical: *Things are going to be a little bit different now. It's not going to be a one-man show anymore. Tommy's just gonna have to get used to it.* I had exerted real leadership, I thought, and I was proud of it.

Slowly, my artificial self-assurances began to fade. I knew my hard-nosed brother better than most. He'd never backed down from a fight in his life. What would make him do so this time? And why would he back down from me?

*T*he following Monday morning, I was settling down to work in my office when my phone rang. It was Don's wife, Terri.

"Douglas, can you come over to the house *right now?* Donnie and I need to show you something." She sounded worried.

I liked my sister-in-law, but I thought she overreacted a lot. "Terri, I'm kind of busy right now, what is it?" It was Monday morning and I wasn't in the mood for histrionics.

"Donnie's got a fax here that says Tommy's sued you."

"Oh come on now," I tried to laugh. "Tommy's not gonna sue me. If anyone had sued me, I'd be the first to know about it, wouldn't I?"

"Look man, I'm just telling you what this piece of paper says," Terri replied.

"What exactly does it say? Read it to me." I tried to sound cool, but I was starting to feel uneasy.

"In the Delaware Court of Chancery," Terri began reading, "Thomas versus Douglas D Box and Box Brothers Holding Company—"

Five minutes later I was at her house. Sure enough, Tom had sued me.

Chapter 32

THE DUNCES OF DELAWARE

I couldn't believe it. *My own brother suing me?* I was trying to solve a dispute, not start a new one. If I'd had any idea this might happen, I wouldn't have gone anywhere near the telephonic board meeting.

In addition to filing suit, Tom had unilaterally removed me as one of four directors and added two of his closest associates to the board of BBHC. This gave him control over three out of the five votes. He was stacking the board against his own family.

My brother may have felt that tightening his grip over the company was justified in order to keep it from being sold. His actions had just the opposite effect. Before the lawsuit, Don, Gary, and I were simply interested in *considering* a sale of the business. After we got into litigation, we became thoroughly determined to sell, no matter what.

The most disturbing aspect of the case for me was my own set of emotions. Compared to Tom, I had always felt subordinate. For years, these remembrances lay submerged on the ocean floor of my subconscious mind like a sunken ship. With the lawsuit, all at once they rose to the surface. It was overwhelming, as if all the old hurts and wounds of childhood, their scabs long since hardened, were opened raw again. I became completely focused on winning at all costs, believing that if I prevailed there would be some sort of prize waiting for me at the end.

The intensity of my resentment, anger, and grief surprised even me. I was so filled with fury that I became more determined to beat my own brother than I believe even Simplot was. I had to stand up to this. I would never be able to live with myself if I didn't.

I told my lawyers to countersue.

*T*om's **lawsuit and** my countersuit boiled down to one simple issue: did a valid board of directors meeting take place on February 15, 1994? That was the date when, in the midst of working out the details of the February Transaction, Don called into the office from someplace near St. Bart's. He spoke to both me and Tom, and we briefly touched on the issuance of the one "A" share. Gary was not on the call or in the office that day.

In his lawsuit, Tom claimed that this conversation rose to the level of a board meeting, that a quorum of directors had been present, and that the board had thereby voted to distribute one share of class "A" to him as the trustee in accordance with our father's will.

Even in Delaware, renowned for its swift corporate justice, the suit dragged on for eighteen months. Toward the beginning of the case, Don treated me as nothing less than his champion, his darling little brother who could do no wrong. He had good cause for treating me this way. I was the sole defendant in the case. If I had wanted to, I could have bailed out at any time and simply capitulated to Tom's claim. Unless Don or Gary intervened—an unlikely scenario—bailing out would effectively ratify Tom's share. Out of concern for my own self-interest as well as fairness to all of my brothers, I chose not to do this.

Although I was the one being sued, I had nothing to do with the "A" share's creation. My name wasn't on it. Yet I was the one racking up hundreds of thousands of dollars in attorneys' fees in Delaware and Texas. While Delaware law is strong in its indemnification provisions, I was fully aware that if I lost, I would face another uphill battle over payment of those fees. I was afraid that I might have to take personal bankruptcy if I lost.

Don didn't have such concerns. His name was not on the petition, and he wasn't racking up *any* legal fees. Even though he did participate as a deponent and a witness, my eldest brother had little to worry about. The lawsuit between his two younger brothers was like having a ringside seat to the biggest boxing match in town, and Don was tickled pink that I was willing to fight this battle for him.

As narrowly defined as the issue appeared on the surface, the litigation process was like gasoline poured on an open fire. The lawsuit drove everyone into a "scorched earth" mindset that felt more akin to civil war than civil procedure. After the lawsuit in Delaware, none of the brothers—myself included—ever seemed capable of making another sound decision. We were so full of fury that we literally couldn't think straight.

Things got so out of hand that at one point, Don and I reverted to adolescent behavior. As we sat nursing our coffee in his office one day, I came up with a silly idea to record a bunch of songs on a cassette tape as a way of mocking the power struggle we were in. If we won, we'd play the tape on the office Muzak system. We'd change the locks on the closet door where the sound system was kept so that Tom's people couldn't turn it off. Everyone would have to listen to our songs all day and we'd have a good laugh.

Don and I came up with a playlist that included songs like "I Just

228 | TEXAS PATRIARCH

Can't Wait to Be King" from *The Lion King*, "The End" by The Doors, and Dylan's "Positively 4th Street." We had a good snicker about it, and then I never gave it another thought.

Although Don and I got along well in the beginning, the closer we got to the end of the case, the more trouble I had with him. I wasn't the only one. He even lost his cool with his longtime secretary. A single mother with two young sons, she was aware of our dispute and worried about what might happen to her employment in the aftermath of a family feud. Fearing that her future might be in jeopardy if she continued to work directly for Don, she asked to be transferred away from his department.

When Don heard her request, he went bananas. Thank goodness I was not privy to what he said to her, but whatever it was must have been some pretty stout language. She retaliated by hiring a lawyer and threatening to file a claim of sexual harassment against Box Energy. The company paid her a six-figure settlement, and she went away.

Don held Tommy accountable for this incident as well.

Not long after, Don and I began to argue about the prospect of firing Tom in the event that we won the case. My lawyers in Delaware, whom I had great respect for, were dead set against it. They said we'd look like *Dumb and Dumber* if we fired our brother.

It sure seemed to me that Don wanted Tom's head. Every time I tried to broach the topic of Tom's continued employment, Don would go ballistic. A number of heated arguments followed.

"Doug, if we win this thing, you gotta realize that you just can't keep Tommy around here," he would lecture me. "He'll obstruct everything we're trying to do."

"Okay, but what do we get out of firing him?" I'd ask.

"We get rid of his sorry ass, that's what!" Don replied.

"Don, think about it. He's a lawyer; he'll be out of a job. He won't have anything else to do but sue us."

"That's *his* problem."

"No, it's going to be *our* problem. The guys up in Delaware think it's a dumb idea. They say it makes us look stupid."

"Those guys don't live down here with these shit-for-brains morons. They don't have any idea the kind of bullshit we have to put up with on a day-to-day basis."

Although Don was getting harder and harder for me to deal with, I was determined to remain on his good side. I was afraid that if our fragile alliance fell apart, we would never get anything done. The business press was scrutinizing our story, and I worried that if the papers caught wind of a rift between Don and me, we'd be made out to look like a bunch of lunatics.

I came up with a compromise. Assuming that the ruling went our way, we'd name the current VP of operations the interim CEO and let Tom head up the legal department, a job he was eminently qualified for. Tom would remain on the board of Box Energy and he would be a one-fourth controlling stockholder of BBHC, like the rest of us. In exchange for this "reassignment of duties," he would agree not to appeal. If we ended up keeping the company, we would announce a comprehensive search for a new, nonfamily CEO. If we opted to sell out, so be it; at least we'd have some money, and it wouldn't matter who the CEO was.

Don wouldn't have it.

I remember the turning point in our relationship. He came to see me one day and sat down on a little blue couch in my office.

"Lad, I think I've come up with a brilliant idea." He smiled at me. "I think the time has come for you to become the president of Box Energy, and I'll be the new CEO."

I took a deep breath and said one of the hardest things I've ever had to say. "I don't think I'm qualified to be president, Don. And to be honest, I don't think you're qualified to be the CEO."

He looked at me as if I had just plunged a dagger into his chest. "But why?" he groaned.

I'd hurt him, but there was no turning back now. "You know I think you're a smart guy, Don, but I just don't see you in that role. You haven't been doing this kind of work for a long time, and you've spent the last five years working on the racetrack."

"Well, I must say that I find myself utterly perplexed by the logic of your thought process, lad," Don replied. "I'm a smart guy—I went to Penn."

He just sat there on my couch, looking down at the floor. Our relationship was never the same.

The longer the Delaware suit wore on, the more deeply entrenched Tom and I grew in our respective positions. Even though we worked in the same office, we didn't speak to each other throughout the entire ordeal of eighteen months.

My feeble efforts to kick-start settlement talks with Tommy went nowhere. Both of us fell into the trap of thinking that we were going to win. But no one wins when a business family goes to court. The only way for us to win would have been to settle the case and fire all the lawyers. Our only real hope of hanging onto the business was to hang on to each other.

Finally, on the afternoon of February 15, 1996, I got a call from my head litigator in Delaware. "Hey Doug, I'm just giving you a heads-up. The court is about to release its opinion in *Box v. Box*. We wanted to get ahold of you so you could be on standby. We'll call you back in about forty-five minutes."

I hung up the phone, closed the door to my office, and asked my secretary to bring me a cup of decaf, thinking this would calm my jitters. The coffee did nothing for me. My heart began to race: *What if I lose this thing?* I knew good and well I'd have trouble paying my exorbitant attorneys' fees. *What if I win this thing?* With Don and I unable to agree on much of anything, we were woefully unprepared to take over. Even though we'd had eighteen months to ponder the various possibilities, with the ruling set to come out in forty-five minutes, I realized that we barely had any plan at all.

At about 4:15 p.m. my phone rang again. It was my Delaware counsel calling back.

"Is this Douglas Box, one of the four directors of Box Brothers Holding Company?"

I was so nervous I didn't take his meaning. "What did you say?"

"We won," said my counsel.

"We won? Really?"

"Yep, you won. Well, technically you lost. You both lost. The court ruled against both you and Tom, saying that there's no outstanding voting stock. Tom's share is no good, and your three new shares are no good either."

"So now what?" I asked.

"Now you get to do whatever you want."

*T*he next morning was a Friday. I took the elevator up to my office on the sixth floor. As soon as the doors opened, I recognized the dirge "The End" from *Apocalypse Now* blaring throughout the office sound system.

Oh my God!

I barely even remembered the practical joke I'd shared with Don months before, but he'd recorded all of the songs we'd listed at his office and added a bunch of his own to boot. He'd changed the locks on the closet door, just as we'd talked about, and hooked up a cassette player to the Muzak system. He also went around the office and manually turned up all the individual speakers.

I felt like Chevy Chase in the famous scene from *Christmas Vacation* when he learns that his brother-in-law has abducted his boss for not paying a year-end bonus. A number of employees from the accounting department came around to sneer at me, thinking that I was behind the whole thing. They had a point.

In the background I could hear the voice of Jim Morrison singing: "*I'll never look into your eyes—again.*"

Chapter 33

REDEMPTION AT THE
FIFTH CIRCUIT

Three weeks later, Tom filed an appeal against the ruling to the Delaware Supreme Court. This meant the matter couldn't be considered final pending the outcome of his appeal, which could take another year.

My initial euphoria wilted pretty fast after I learned of the appeal. I'd been lobbying to protect Tom's job as CEO, but now he had taken away a lot of my leverage. Because of technicalities related to how carefully the opinion had been written, the ruling could not be appealed. When Tom chose to appeal it anyway, it made it impossible for me to defend him much further.

A week or so after the Delaware ruling, Don and I called a meeting of the board of directors of BBHC. All four of us attended that meeting with a bunch of lawyers huddled around. It was a horrible meeting, not much better than the telephonic board meeting. Don, Gary, and I voted to issue ourselves eleven voting shares each, but no shares to Tom. The decision not to issue voting shares to Tom was in retaliation for his appeal.

In the long run, this would not be a good decision. Things were getting worse, not better.

The thirty-three shares were held in three separate trusts, and Don, Gary, and I served as co-trustees for all three trusts. The trust agreements stipulated that two out of the three trustees could act on behalf of each trust so long as it didn't constitute a breach of fiduciary duty.

Don and Gary agreed to name me president of BBHC. I suppose this was their way of rewarding me for having "won" the lawsuit, but in practice, the high-ranking title didn't mean a thing to my oldest brother. I was seven years his junior. I wasn't smart enough to get into St. Mark's, I hadn't attended an Ivy League, and I didn't have an MBA. Don wasn't about to defer to me on much of anything. He had already been upstaged by one younger brother; he wasn't about to let it happen again.

Still, as president, I could finally work on getting us out of our legal entanglements. The first thing I did after winning the Delaware lawsuit was to interview some investment banking firms to consider putting the company in play. This would hopefully drive the lagging share price up and force Mr. Simplot to raise his bid accordingly. I wanted to put an end to the ten-year battle with Simplot, and I didn't think my brothers and I had the capacity to work together. I wasn't necessarily opposed to keeping Box Energy rather than selling it, but if we did keep it, I wanted a new, nonfamily CEO to run it. I told Don and his lawyers this all along, never wavering in my opinion.

I erroneously thought that winning the case in Delaware would restore some of Don's lost composure. I was hoping it would reestablish a sense of equanimity in him, and I was anxious for the erudite scholar who'd once led a board meeting in prayer to return. But even after I won the lawsuit, Don's temperament continued to steadily decline.

One of the most bizarre things he ever did was to file a fresh lawsuit against Tom, seeking to have him disbarred. He wanted me to join him as a co-plaintiff, but I vehemently told him no. I began to have serious doubts about Don's mental well-being. Was he really mad at Tommy, or was he taking out his hostilities on his deceased father for the blessing he'd never received? I had to wonder what was really going on with him.

Prior to the ruling, my alliance with my oldest brother had been cemented by a so-called "common enemy." We were united in our struggle to undo the one "A" share. Once the ruling came out, however, the "common enemy" vanished, and our relationship grew more volatile.

Given his erratic mindset, I grew concerned that if I disagreed with any little thing he wanted to do, our coalition would fall apart. If that happened, I feared total chaos would reign. I was already walking on eggshells after I told him I didn't think he was an ideal CEO, but he was making it harder and harder to maintain a tenuous peace. I was nevertheless determined to stay on good terms with him, regardless of what it cost.

/n May 1996, I got a call on my cell phone from Rock. "Doug, there's a guy out here at the nineteenth hole who says that the Fifth Circuit has ruled in the Simplot case. He's trying to figure out what it means."

What it meant was that Tom's finest hour had arrived. It was the moment he'd waited on for four long years.

Tom and his team of lawyers had worked hard on the appeal of the Simplot case to the Fifth Circuit in New Orleans. Years earlier, they'd found a prominent law school professor from Harvard who had a noted reputation for only taking cases he was sure to win.

When the professor reviewed our case and accepted the assignment, Tom was convinced that it was only a matter of time. After reading the brief several times myself, I came to believe that Tom was right. We did have a chance.

The court ruled exactly as our lawyers had hoped. It reversed the original decision and remanded the case back down to the lower court for a new trial due to the jury's inconsistent answers to the liability issues. It also vacated the constructive trust over the lucrative pipeline.

Everyone was euphoric. Everyone, that is, except Tom. The court had given him the win he wanted, but it came far too late. He subsequently confessed to me that instead of celebrating loudly, as Don and I did that night, he drove over to Dad's gravesite at Sparkman Hillcrest to report the win to his fallen hero.

No one was surprised when Simplot next appealed to the US Supreme Court. Not a single one of our lawyers had any concern about that. Six months later, the high court released a statement that it would not hear the appeal.

Simplot had lost.

But so had we.

*E*ven after our big win, Don still insisted that Box Energy fire Tom as the CEO. The board refused, taking the position that the family feud, though unfortunate, had little to do with the management of the company. They respected and trusted Tom. They didn't seem to respect Don.

In response, Don took the drastic measure of threatening to fire the entire board of Box Energy. He insisted that I sign a unanimous consent as president to replace all but one of the directors of the company. I told him that I thought we should take the high road in dealing with Tom, but after I'd told Don that I didn't think he was a CEO, he never listened to another word I said.

Recruiting a new set of directors took months. As we went about the process of vetting the new director candidates, Don's oratory prowess was on full display. He had a knack for conversation, and listening to him make his arguments was like hearing a stirring lecture from a brilliant professor. But over time, his loquaciousness made me weary. It reminded me of a funny expression that Aunt Jan used when describing people who liked to talk too much: diarrhea of the mouth.

After Don's new board was seated, his first order of business was to insist that they fire Tom and two of his closest associates, his CFO and a recently hired public relations expert.

Unlike Don's handsome exit package, Tom received no severance. Forced to vacate the only job he ever wanted, Tom would never again set foot in our father's office. Though he'd had trouble leading the family, Tom did everything his father had ever asked him to do.

Eerily reminiscent of the manner in which Don was severed from Box Energy, the new board's firing of Tom struck me as a bit naïve and cavalier. I don't think it was possible for any of us to know just how destabilizing their action would become.

Given Don's pattern of avoiding conflict, I was the one who had to break the news to Mother. The newspapers were tracking the story pretty closely, and I didn't want her to learn of Tom's firing from someone else.

"Mom, I want to bring you up to date with what's going on around here. I know you've been concerned about all the problems we've had. I'm sorry to say that things have really gotten out of hand. I think you ought to know that the company has a new board now. They met today for the first time, and they let Tom go."

All I could hear for a few moments was silence, and then she began to weep. I said what I could to console her. But down deep, I realized I'd let her down. Although privately opposed to Tom's termination, I'd stood by and let it happen, an act of omission I will always regret.

I wasn't proud of what we'd done in removing Tom from power, but at the time, it seemed as though we'd had no choice. And yet when I heard my mother's tears, I knew it had been a mistake. Fern Box was a simple woman, but her heart was always in the right place, especially when it came to her children.

$\mathcal{T}$o my chagrin, on the same day that Tom was fired, Don's new board voted him in as the new CEO. Immediately, a spokesman for the company sent out a press release, declaring the following: "The board of directors is determined to increase shareholder value, but has no intention to seek bids for Box Energy." All of a sudden, Don and his team no longer wanted to sell.

This was news to me.

Previously, the faction led by me, Gary, and Don had consistently and publicly lobbied to sell the business. A number of Wall Street analysts and shareholders had expressed support for the plan, believing that a sale would be the quickest way to profit from an investment in Box Energy. Tom's position, by contrast, had always been that growing the company would be the best way to benefit the shareholders. Now that Don had Tom's old job, this seemed to be his position as well. The irony wasn't lost on the analysts, the papers, or me.

Gregg Jones, a writer for *The Dallas Morning News*, captured it best when he wrote: "The possibility that a sale of Box Energy might not occur dismayed at least one Wall Street analyst who had been recommending shares to investors on the belief that the three allied brothers would put the company on the block. 'I was recommending this company on the premise that it would be worth more in the hands of somebody else,' said Michael Spohn, an analyst for Petroleum Research Group. 'Now it appears to be business as usual with the same last name on the door, and that's not what I was anticipating. That's not a positive for the stock.'"

Following Don's announcement, the NASDAQ-traded shares of Box Energy closed down fifteen percent.

Chapter 34

DUMB AND
GETTING DUMBER

As soon as Don became CEO, he got busy firing a number of long-time employees of the company. Some of them had admirably served under my father for years. Now they were being unceremoniously dumped for no other reason than the perception that they were too close to Tom.

Don fired our long-standing audit firm, Coopers & Lybrand, simply because one of their local partners had agreed to appear in court as a friendly witness to Tom. Letting our auditors go seemed drastic to me. And yet, again, I stood by and let it happen. Arthur Andersen became the new audit firm.

Don also began to remodel his own office to meet his personal preferences and tastes. Having finally wrested control of the enterprise from his younger, more charismatic brother, he found that he liked the feeling of power. He enjoyed the newfound attention that accompanied it, too. The smiles from the girls in the office seemed bigger, more seductive. Don took to peacocking around the office, proclaiming: "It's good to be king!"

Unfortunately, Don's tenure as CEO was destined to be short-lived. Aside from administration, which he took to with characteristic lethargy, his only real background in the business had been selling refined products out of our old Okmulgee refinery, a business segment we'd abandoned some twenty years before, after the liquidation of OKC.

My oldest brother hadn't had a real boss in years. He wasn't used to working or to being held accountable. Now with an eager new board in place, he had a lot more on his plate, and he didn't take to it well.

Tom didn't take well to being fired, either. He immediately hired a gladiator-style law firm and directed them to file two fresh lawsuits for wrongful termination, one in state court and another in federal court. He sued Don, Gary, and me as individuals. He also sued Box Energy, as well as each of the seven new directors of the new board.

Although Gary's involvement was limited, the Delaware lawsuit had been hard on him. As one of the four directors of BBHC, he'd had to give a lengthy deposition and testify during the trial in Delaware. He didn't like having to show up in court against Tom, the brother he'd always been closest to.

He only agreed to cooperate with us in exchange for our promise to "clean everything up." Now that it had been almost a year after the Delaware decision, Gary wasn't seeing anything getting cleaned up. He was seeing things get worse.

Tom's firing did not sit well with Gary. The two middle brothers out of the four, they were closest in age as well as sentiment. The shade tree mechanic had respect for the way Tom could handle a gun, throw a knife, and catch northern pike off the dock at the Thousand Islands.

When we got Gary to testify against Tom in court, we were pushing our luck. Now that Don's new board had fired him, we'd pushed our luck too far.

Even though Gary had almost nothing to do with Tom's dismissal, he now had to defend himself against the two new lawsuits. This required us to retain two more law firms, one to represent the company and the other to represent each of us as individuals. It also meant that Gary would have to talk to more and more lawyers. Gary didn't like talking to lawyers—another good trait he had.

I remember the day he finally snapped. He came storming into my office wearing a ball cap, shorts, and T-shirt, and he threw me a ferocious look. "All you know how to do is sit around and talk to these fucking lawyers all day, charging us $300 an hour!"

The storm had been brewing in his mind for a while now. I wasn't shocked that it was finally breaking, just surprised he'd held on for so long. He'd recently suffered a minor stroke, and from the way he was getting worked up, I was worried he might have another one.

"I thought you said that if you won this stinkin' lawsuit, we'd be able to sell the company and get out of all this bullshit," he went on. "Well, we won the goddamn lawsuit—or you won the lawsuit—or somebody won the lawsuit. Maybe Bozo the Clown won it; I don't know. But *somebody* won the fuckin' lawsuit, and now all we have is more bullshit." He rattled off the various lawsuits on his fingers. "More lawsuits from Tommy, more lawsuits from Simplot, more lawsuits from Trammell Crow." He threw up his hands in frustration. "More lawsuits from shit-knows-who. We've been jerked around for years, and nothing's happening. What the fuck is Don doing? He wants to sit up there and drink coffee all day and talk to his secretaries while we're jerking around down here getting sued and paying lawyers. I'm sick of the lawyers. Sick of 'em all! Why don't we just sell the company to Simplot and tell Don we ain't waiting around no more?"

"That'd be okay by me," I said. "That's what I wanted to do in the first place. That's what Don said *he* wanted to do. But after he became CEO, I guess he's changed his mind."

Gary was fed up. He was ready to do something. He wasn't sure what it was, but it had to happen soon. "If we don't do something pretty quick, next thing you know we'll be sitting here next year having this same conversation."

Just then an idea popped into my head.

"You know what we could do," I began. "You could sign a power of attorney over to me so that I could vote your stock for the purpose of pursuing a sale. Then I could see if Simplot will talk to me. Alone, they'll say I can't deliver anything, but if I tell them I have your vote, they might deal with me." I tried to sound nonchalant. "We can try that and see if it goes anywhere. If it doesn't, we can just tear up the power of attorney."

Gary sighed. "Well, I guess it's better than sitting around here talking to lawyers all day."

I had a document drafted up that gave me the power to deal with Gary's shares, including the ability to vote them for the purpose of pursuing a sale of the company. The three-page document was fully revocable by Gary at any time. Gary and I both signed it, but I didn't let him keep a copy. I didn't tell anyone else about it, not even Don. Given how the letter I'd written to Tom had ended up in *The Wall Street Journal*, I didn't want Gary's power of attorney getting into the wrong hands.

But my plans to keep it a secret ended shortly after Gary told his wife, Rhonda, who liked to be apprised of everything that was going on in her husband's life. She may not have appreciated my doing something with Gary's stock without her knowledge. She called my office and asked my assistant to produce a copy for her. My assistant did so, with my approval, but then she inadvertently left the original face down on the Xerox machine.

I couldn't help but think about Benjamin Franklin's famous expression: three people can keep a secret as long as two of them are dead.

A few minutes later, one of Don's racetrack buddies came into the copy room, lifted up the copier lid, and found the document, which was titled "Revocable Power of Attorney." Instead of returning the document to me, I imagine he sprinted all the way back down the hallway to Don's office and handed it to him, out of breath.

I had just given Don an excuse to go after me, and that's exactly what he did.

*M*eanwhile, my oldest brother was learning the hard way what it meant when people said, "Be careful what you wish for." His hand-picked board, whom he'd spoken of so affectionately just a few months earlier, was rebelling against him. Two of his choice directors resigned, and a third was threatening to do so. The remaining directors looked to me for guidance. I told them to act like a board and take whatever action they felt would be in the best interest of all the stockholders. If that meant hiring a new CEO, so be it. I had been unwilling to protect Tom's job, so why should I protect Don's any longer?

As the nominal new head of BBHC, my biggest objective was to settle with Simplot. Now that I had some authority, I began pushing toward that goal. I told the lawyers I wanted a face-to-face mediation with Mr. Simplot in Dallas. It took months of planning to make this happen, but finally, a date was set.

The mediation took place at Rock's office in downtown Dallas. When I arrived that morning, Mr. Simplot and his entourage were gathered in the lobby. I walked over and introduced myself. Mr. Simplot and I shook hands. He looked me right in my eyes and said, "I'm ready to settle."

All the stories I'd heard about Mr. Simplot didn't resonate with me that day. He certainly struck me as a strong man, a skilled negotiator, and a tough customer, but I didn't discern anything untoward about him. My overall impression of Mr. Simplot was that he was simply a very serious and successful businessman.

During the ten-hour mediation that followed, Rock and I worked hard to carve out a settlement. Ironically, in the end our offer was identical to the deal that Simplot and Dad had worked on years ago. Sitting across the table from the self-made billionaire, encountering the same obstacles Dad had encountered in him, I felt strangely connected to my father again. I needed him now. It made me miss him.

Alas, the mediation concluded without agreement. Following the day and a half session, I was exhausted and upset that we couldn't settle. I thought: *I guess this is what killed my father.*

Later on, I learned that the mediation had been rigged against me in advance. In retaliation for my power of attorney over Gary's shares, Don had his lawyers inform Simplot's lawyers that he would refuse to go along with any agreement we reached during the mediation, regardless of the outcome.

Somehow I don't think that Don wanted to see our family survive. He was fighting with his brothers, but it seemed to me he was really trying to get back at his father in some way.

Whatever his reasons, his sabotage of the mediation with Simplot signaled another turning point in my relationship with Don. Once he figured out that I was no longer playing by his rules, he went to work on Gary. He told Gary that I was the bad guy now, that I was telling the board that the company needed a new, nonfamily CEO. Moreover, I was deliberately undermining all of the good things that Don was doing at the company. He pointed to the power of attorney as proof. Don told Gary that rather than using the revocable power of attorney as I'd promised Gary I would—to negotiate with Simplot, and nothing more—I had instead used it to manipulate the directors of Box Energy and undermine Don's authority as CEO. According to Don, I had told the directors that they didn't need to listen to Don anymore; they only needed to listen to me. Don convinced Gary that nothing good could come of our situation as long as he did not have full and complete control over the enterprise.

"Doug and Rock are out to destroy this company, Gary," Don would say. "Our only chance is to get rid of those worthless bastards."

Working with his racetrack buddies along with yet another attorney, Don came up with a fraudulent transaction to buy Gary's voting shares. Doing so would give him 2/3 of all the outstanding voting shares, leaving me in a minority position of 1/3. All of it went on behind my back.

The deal that Don coaxed Gary into was this: Gary would continue to receive his current salary until Don could raise the funds to buy him out in full. The whole scheme was in violation of a trust agreement between the three of us, and in being a party to it, Gary would be making a prima facie breach of fiduciary duty. No attorney would have advised Gary to do it.

I remember the day that I opened the oversized envelope and saw the two-inch thick set of documents that Don had put together to buy Gary's voting stock. None of those who were involved in putting it together had the nerve to present it to me in person. They hired a mail courier to hand deliver the package to me at my office.

The letter explained that Don and Gary had decided to join forces and consolidate their ownership under a new LLC, one that Don would have sole control over. As a requirement under Delaware law, Don filed suit against me in the same Delaware Court of Chancery venue that Tom sued me two years earlier.

I gaped in astonishment at the documents set before me. I couldn't believe it. I stared at the papers for so long that the inside of my mouth got dry. I'd never felt this bad before. It was hard for me to speak or swallow. I wondered if I was having a stroke like Gary had just a few months before.

I had no one to turn to. Don had turned Gary against me now, and I was too embarrassed to call Tommy and admit what happened. I was afraid he might say, "See, I told you so." I couldn't tell any of the employees what had happened because the story might get leaked to the press.

I got in my car and drove away from the office. I knew that Rock was out of town, so I tried to call one of my other lawyers. He came on the line, but I couldn't say anything because my mouth was too dry. I'd never had cottonmouth like that before. I hung up and drove home.

I felt a little better when I got home. I fixed myself a Coke and petted my dog. I tried to call Don and his racetrack buddy. They were nowhere to be found. I presume they were off hiding somewhere. But I had the cover letter from the lawyer who had drafted all the documents. I picked up the phone and dialed his office number. His assistant said he wasn't in, so I left a message on his voice mail. I stated that I was in receipt of the documents he'd prepared and that I intended to sue him personally. I hung up. He never returned that phone call.

I never followed through on my threat to sue him—too bad.

This was the meltdown that I had feared all along. Knowing how tenuous my alliance was with Don, I stood by and let him do everything he wanted. I'd handed him the company on a golden platter, and then I stood by and let him fire the brother I'd always been closest to. Now it was just a matter of time before everything would devolve into utter chaos and disorder.

Don's team may have tried to deemphasize to Gary that Delaware law required them to file a new lawsuit against me, identical to the one that Tom had filed against me years before. They knew Gary wouldn't like the idea. But once Gary learned that Don was indeed suing me, he lost all patience with Don's deal, and in a comical display of turnabout, he switched his allegiance back to me.

Gary then tried to rescind the entire transaction by invoking an oral promise that Don had used to persuade Gary to sign the papers. If Gary changed his mind *for any reason*, Don had proposed out loud to him, Don would gladly reverse the entire stock transfer agreement. After Gary changed his mind about the deal, he called Don's bluff and told him he wanted to recant the sale of his shares. Don scoffed at him and refused.

A week later, for the first time ever, Gary hired a law firm of his own—the Hartnett Law Firm of Dallas (itself a family business). Once the Hartnett firm was retained, all hell broke loose—again.

Their first order of business was to sue Don for fraud.

Gary was suing Don to rescind the stock purchase. Don countersued Gary. Don was suing me in Delaware to consolidate his control. I was suing Don for the breach of fiduciary duty under the trust agreement. Don had already filed a frivolous lawsuit to have Tom disbarred. Tom was suing Don, Gary, and me for wrongful termination in state court. Tom was suing Don, Gary, and me for wrongful termination in federal court, and Tom was suing every individual director on the new board of Box Energy who had fired him.

It was nothing short of a bloodbath.

How could it ever end?

Chapter 35

FROM RICHES TO RAGS

There are few people who have more power than a federal judge. They do not run for election. They're appointed to the bench for life by the president of the United States. That means they never have to worry much about the unpopularity of their decisions.

Tom's hasty termination and his subsequent lawsuit put us directly in the crosshairs of a federal judge named Joseph A. Kendall. If Tom had not been fired, the federal court would have had no jurisdiction over our case.

In January 1997, Judge Kendall ordered all four of us into his private chambers for a settlement conference at the federal courthouse in downtown Dallas.

My brothers and I and our respective counsel filed into the conference room, avoiding eye contact with one another. As we took seats at the large oval table, Gary whispered animatedly to his lawyer. During happier times, the rest of us used to joke that anytime we saw Gary in a suit, someone was getting either married or buried. Today, there were no jokes between us.

The lawyers scrambled to put away their cell phones, and we all rose in deference as the judge strode into the conference room. "Come on, guys, this is a settlement conference," the judge said, waving us back down. "You don't need to stand up."

Judge Kendall had been a police officer prior to going into the judiciary, and his biceps bulged beneath the fabric of his dress shirt. He wasn't a large man, but he seemed taller due to the robust authority he exuded. It was easy for me to imagine this scrappy former street cop imposing his will on criminals twice his size, a pistol replacing the index finger he waved at us now. He was unorthodox, unpredictable, and controversial, and the fate of our family was in his hands.

And as we were all about to learn, Judge Kendall had a bigger agenda in mind than simply adjudicating Tom's wrongful termination lawsuit.

"Here's what we're gonna do with this." Sitting down, he crossed his arms over his chest and looked around the table at the four of us. "I'm tired of listening to the lawyers," he began. "I've been hearing from them for a while now about the mess your family's business is in. We all know they'd be happy to keep on talking and billing y'all for years to come." Judge Kendall cracked a wry smile. "So what I want now," he continued, "is to hear from you guys—the four brothers."

One of the lawyers tried to interject, but the judge shut him down. "I really don't have any interest in what you have to say, Counselor. I want to hear from each of the brothers. One at a time, I want to hear each of you give me your version of what's going on here."

I wanted to high-five him.

Don was first. The ink had barely dried on his fraudulent transfer of Gary's stock. Looking guilty, he blustered about his birthright as the eldest son. "Well, these young lads here, they're all a bunch of real nice guys, but I've been here the longest. I'm a real smart guy, and we're doing everything right with the company now. It's just tough to convince my little brothers 'cause they just don't seem to understand."

Judge Kendall seemed puzzled.

During his turn, Tom spoke in a forceful but calm voice. "Your Honor, all I want to do is run the business that my father left me in charge of and restore a part of his legacy. That's all I'm trying to do. These guys fired me so that they could sell the business. I'm vehemently opposed to that. The dispute set before us today is actually an outgrowth of a lawsuit that took place a year ago. Unfortunately, we ended up in court, and I lost. Now they're running a vendetta against me, trying to kick me out." Tom sounded righteously indignant as his voice echoed throughout the room.

The judge nodded.

Gary went next. He was much more emotional, and took no care to sugarcoat his feelings. "This goddamn business bullshit is killin' me, Judge. I mean it; I'm not just exaggerating. It's *killin'* me." Gary's head jutted forward and his eyes bugged out as he drove home his point. "Six months ago I had a *stroke*, for Chrissakes! You know what caused that? Stress." He threw his hands up, disgust flashing in his eyes. "That's what did it, Judge, plain and simple. Stupid, petty arguments about money that stressed me out so bad I had a goddamned stroke."

The judged looked dismayed as Gary finished his impassioned tale.

Finally it was my turn.

"Your Honor," I began.

"You don't have to say 'Your Honor,'" the judge interrupted me. "We're not in court today. This is a settlement conference."

His attempt to put me at ease did little to lighten my mood, and I stumbled over my words as I spoke. "The way I see things is this. If we can't all get along, we should just sell the company and get on with our lives before we ruin the business and destroy our family. If we don't sell the company, we should bring in an outside CEO to run the thing so that we don't fight over it."

Judge Kendall smiled. "Now, that doesn't seem like such an unreasonable approach, does it?" He turned to the others. "Guys, what's wrong with Doug's idea?"

I wanted to hug him, but as for my brothers, there was virtually no response. Gary was spent and said nothing. Tom also stayed quiet, because his lawyer wouldn't allow him to utter another word. Don finally mumbled, "That's what we're trying to do, is bring in an outside president."

The judge sat in silence for a few moments, pondering what he'd heard. The tension in the room grew with each passing second.

"Thank you, gentleman," he finally said. "I'm glad to know where each of you stands at this juncture."

He tapped his fingers on the table.

"You know," he went on, "life's funny. I knew Cloyce Box. I knew him personally. When I first got out of law school, I was broke and needed a job. Your dad gave me some work, and that meant a lot to me. I'll always be grateful to him for that. Your father was a great man. He did things to help people that most people never even knew about. I have a lot of respect for your dad."

Judge Kendall stopped and looked from Don, to Gary, to Tom, and then to me. "But you guys are a disgrace to him."

He paused to let the rebuke sink in. I shrank down in my chair.

"So here's what I want y'all to do," he said. "I want y'all to settle the case."

Tom's lawyer tried to object, but Judge Kendall held up a hand. "Listen up," he insisted. "I've been following this thing in the papers and I know that you've been going at this for a long time now." He frowned. "Too long. I care about you guys because I knew your father, and I'm worried for y'all. You can't believe the liability you can get into with these public stockholders, and this family feud of yours is all over the street. The industry vultures are sitting back, just waiting to pick up whatever's left of your business after the four of you finally drive it into the ditch. The ultimate winners will be the lawyers. The losers will be you and your families."

This wasn't the judge's first rodeo. He knew the inevitable outcome. "But y'all still have some options," he continued. "The obvious answer would be for one or more of you to buy the others out at a fair price."

That sounded like a great plan to me. Don had the look of a deer caught in headlights. Gary nodded vigorously. But Tom's expression was hard.

"Whatever you gentlemen decide," Judge Kendall concluded, "I urge you to put animosity aside and start making business decisions as opposed to emotional ones. But let's not forget: beyond doing business together, y'all are still brothers. Once this thing is settled one way or another, how are you ever going to be a family again?"

With that, the settlement conference was over. Judge Kendall pushed his chair back and stood up. As he made his way toward the door, Tom's lawyer straightened up in his chair and finally took his opportunity to shoot back.

"With all due respect, Your Honor," he said, "you can't make us settle this case!"

Judge Kendall stopped and peered over at the lawyer who had just barked at him.

"No, I can't make you settle the case," he conceded. "But I sure can make you wish you had."

*A*fter the conference, we learned what Judge Kendall had meant by that final remark. He sent out a motion that threatened to appoint a federal receiver over all of our assets. As our attorneys explained, the receiver's job would be to liquidate the assets of the company, pay off any and all creditors, and distribute whatever proceeds remained to the stockholders. The receiver's actions would be accountable to only the federal court. The judge ordered each of us brothers to submit the names of three people who might be good candidates to become the receiver for BBHC. This order forced us to think, in detail, about what life might be like for us if Kendall actually *did* appoint a receiver.

Even though Judge Kendall never actually appointed a receiver, as a practical matter, he didn't need to. The threat of receivership was just as powerful, and it sent all four of us into a scramble.

A few days later I got a call from Mom. Her voice had a tone I recognized from the past. It was the same one she used when she'd told me about Dad's affair with Jane Palmer.

"Douglas, can you come over to my house for a meeting?" I knew she meant business.

"You mean, right now?"

"Yes, right now. I have Tommy and Don over here, and they're talking about how to settle everything."

"Settle everything, what do you mean?" I paused. "Wait, did you say Tommy and Don are over at your house?"

"Yes, and we need to get ahold of Gary, too. I want all four of you boys together right here in my house. I want to see if we can work all this out," she said.

I was incredulous. Even before Dad died I had tried to get my brothers to be more reasonable. They didn't seem to want to listen much. Now they were both in trouble. Tom had been kicked completely out of the company, and Don was facing the prospect of a federal receiver kicking him out as well.

It made me more than a little peeved. *Now that there's a federal judge breathing down their necks,* I thought, *all of a sudden everyone's ready to act all nice in front of Mom.* I felt like saying something spiteful to her. I'm glad I didn't.

"I haven't had lunch yet," I said instead. "I'm gonna pick up a bucket of fried chicken and eat it over there. If anyone else is hungry, they can eat with me too," I said.

With that, we hung up, and I got ready to meet all of my brothers face-to-face. No courtrooms, no office politics, no lawyers. How long had it been, I wondered suddenly, since all of us had done that?

*W*hen I arrived at Mom's house, I found Tom, Don, and Gary all seated around a small table in her breakfast room. Tom looked relaxed but strong. Don looked pale and shaken. Gary looked unusually calm and patient.

It was the first time I'd seen all of my brothers seated around the same kitchen table in years.

I pulled up a chair and popped open the bucket of fried chicken and rolls. Mom jumped up to fetch us some cold drinks from the fridge, like she used to do when we ate around that little table at our house on Park Lane, before the ranch, before Dad's business empire. Memories of meals we'd shared during childhood made me ache for those carefree days. We didn't know it back then, I realized, but we were a wealthy family. We didn't have much money, but we had the kind of wealth money can't buy.

With Mom close at hand and all the lawyers out of the room, we were able to make a ton of headway. We discussed ideas about how we could keep the company and continue to work together. It all seemed to come together so easily. Too easily, in fact. We would reinstate Tom as the CEO and let Don and Tom vote the Box Energy stock equally. We'd continue to fend off Simplot using our new leverage at the Fifth Circuit. Most importantly, we agreed, we'd dismiss all of our lawsuits against each other.

At one point, we even went so far as to vow that we'd never so much as speak to another attorney for the rest of our lives.

*B*y the end of that meeting, I was optimistic that we could finally put our differences aside and act like a family again. But within a matter of days, the tentative agreement we'd reached at Mom's house began to break down.

In retrospect, the problem was that none of us was comfortable enough to honestly express our feelings in front of our mother. No one wanted to be seen as the bad guy. I certainly doubted Don's sincerity in allowing Tom to return and take his place as CEO. And even if Don was willing to allow that to happen, how would the market react? On Gary's and my part, we were too bashful to admit in front of our well-meaning mother that we'd rather have a bunch of money than continue battling it out in court day after day, even if that meant the end of Tom's career. And Tom, as I'd learn soon enough, had his own concerns.

Another big obstacle was the attorneys' fees. We owed them a ton of money but weren't sure how we could ever pay them all off. But a transaction with a billionaire would give us the assurances we could arrange for everyone to get paid off at the closing.

In the end, the lure of instant wealth proved the last nail in the coffin. Though I'd grown up in the lap of Texas luxury, I'd never achieved any personal wealth of my own. I'd never had more than $20,000 at any point in my life, and I never had a salary higher than $80,000. My father had been a wealthy man, but he had always been highly leveraged. As illiquid as he was, much of his wealth never felt real.

Nevertheless, I was willing to try to forgo my greedy temptations, but only if everyone was ready, willing, and able to come to an agreement and to do so quickly.

The next day I phoned Tom and asked if he was prepared to follow through on what we'd discussed the day before. He began to demur, and I got upset. I didn't like the way he was speaking to me now, nothing like the tone and attitude of the day before. All the family goodwill seemed to vanish overnight.

I pressed him further and hotly demanded why he was dragging his feet. He stated that he wasn't opposed in principle to dismissing his lawsuits, but that he'd do so only in accordance with his own timetable—not anyone else's.

I exploded.

"Look, all I'm trying to do is save this goddamn company," I said furiously. "If I were you I'd start listening to me because I'm trying to help you. I don't really want to keep this company, but for Mom's sake and everyone else's sake, if we can all agree on something, I might be talked into sticking it out. But you've got to listen to what I'm telling you to do."

"It's my prerogative to proceed as I see fit," he calmly countered.

I was so mad my voice was shaky now. "I'm telling you to call your lawyer right now, tell him we have a settlement, and tell him that you're instructing him to dismiss those two lawsuits. If you don't do it, that's fine by me, but I'm telling you, the company is going to get sold if you don't act *right now*. Do it just like we talked about yesterday at Mom's house!"

"It's my prerogative as to how and when I dismiss my causes of action," he continued. "This is all purely within my control."

"Prerogative? Give me a fucking break, Tommy! You've been kicked out of the company. You don't have any prerogative. You're not in any position to dictate anything here. I'm trying to help you!"

I don't remember the rest, but that conversation didn't end well, and it left me in a sour mood. I called Don and reported to him that I didn't have any faith in our last-minute settlement at Mom's house.

"I just don't see this thing working out," I told Don. "I think we just have to proceed with the sale and get that judge off our back."

Don seemed more than relieved.

"I can't tell you how glad I am to hear you say that, lad. I don't have any faith in the deal at all. In fact, I think it's a stupid deal." He cleared his throat. "Let's sell."

Although I agreed with Don, I knew that Mom would feel disappointed that she couldn't help us resolve things to keep the company and save Tom's job. I realized then that the meeting the day before was little more than a ruse, an artificial display of cordiality for the benefit of our mother.

On August 29, 1997, an army of lawyers gathered in Judge Kendall's federal courtroom. The last time I had seen so many attorneys in one place had been at Dad's funeral. This event was just as somber for my brothers and me. This was not at all the case for the lawyers, one of whom I overheard say, "I wouldn't miss this showdown for the whole world!" Many of his colleagues seemed to agree.

Judge Kendall had ordered us into his court to prove up what became known as the Master Settlement Agreement. The ten-inch-thick set of documents would resolve once and for all the litigation between Simplot and the four brothers simultaneously.

After receiving final approval from the federal court to proceed, we worked late into the night to close this gut-wrenching transaction. We sold Box Brothers Holding Company to a trust controlled by J. R. Simplot and settled ten years of litigation.

Around midnight, I walked out of the attorney's office with a big check in hand. As I drove to the bank the next day to deposit it, I couldn't help but wonder how much of that money was federally insured.

A few nights later, I hired a limousine and took my lawyers and all their spouses to dinner at The Mansion on Turtle Creek, a restaurant known for celebrating special occasions. My attorneys had become like a surrogate family for me when my own had fallen apart. In addition to their professional help, I was grateful for the emotional support they had provided through such a harrowing time. We ate a sumptuous meal and drank expensive wine, savoring our "win" to the fullest. But as the evening wore on, something began to gnaw at me.

Well after midnight, I was the last remaining passenger in the limo. As the chauffeur drove me down the darkened streets to drop me off at my apartment, an early hangover took hold. All the pretentious fun of the evening had vanished. Left alone in the dark, anguish flooded over me. All at once the years of turmoil came crashing through the protective walls of my psyche. The past lay in wreckage behind me, and I was overtaken by a deep wave of regret.

I thought that money would make me a wealthy man, but as the driver pulled up to my front door to let me out, I'd never felt poorer in my life.

I stepped out into the solemn quiet of that dark night, handed the driver an obscenely handsome tip, and bid him farewell.

Epilogue

BOX ROAD

The settlement agreement we reached with Simplot profoundly changed the tenor of the relationships between the four of us Box brothers. One might assume that our newfound wealth would lead us all to a higher spiritual place, but money generally doesn't work that way. I wrongly assumed that selling out would end or at least mitigate the conflict between the four of us. For the most part, it had just the opposite effect.

Five days after we sold the business to Simplot, I began boxing up all my files to move out of my office. Few, if any, employees came around to say good-bye or wish me luck. They'd been instructed by the new owners not to speak to anyone whose last name was Box, or at least that's what they told me. My longtime assistant, however, wept for days leading up to my exit. She got over it, though. As part of selling out, I managed to ensure that she kept her job.

My relationship with Gary was the least impacted by these events because his involvement was minimal. He and I were the only two brothers who didn't sue each other. Gary may have expressed himself a bit too crudely at times, but I give him credit for always being true to himself. Gary wasn't a sophisticated guy, and he never cared for school, but at times he showed more emotional intelligence than all of the rest of us put together. He and his wife, Rhonda, have remained married for thirty-six years.

Tom was already gone from the family business, as the new board had fired him a year earlier.

During the time that the complex deal with Simplot was being hammered out, Don's power grab over Gary's shares enabled him to negotiate directly with the new buyer, Simplot. The rest of us—Tom, Gary, and I—had to contend with Don's lawyers, who, in essence, were brokering the deal. Since we were also embroiled in litigation among ourselves, Don's lawyers were somewhat adverse to us. In negotiating what would become the biggest financial transaction of our lives, we had to agree to be represented by a law firm whose loyalty was to Don.

Don used this to his advantage. In addition to the other monies he received from the sale, Don negotiated an employment contract with the Simplot-controlled entity, which promptly changed its name from Box Energy Corporation to Remington Oil and Gas. The nominal term of the agreement was for two years, but Don worked for Remington for at least five years. In the end, he became an officer and a director, a position that entitled him to receive fresh stock options and numerous other perks that ultimately made him a much wealthier person than Gary, Tom, and me put together.

Nine years after we sold Box Energy for an inputted value of $220 million, the company was sold again for $1.36 billion. A number of factors contributed to such a dramatic turnaround.

Previously traded on the NASDAQ under two classes of stock

(class A and Class B), the settlement that ended the power strug-gle between two of its largest shareholders allowed it to reissue one class of stock. This helped to facilitate a move to the New York Stock Exchange, which made the company more attractive to the institu-tional investment community. A favorable ruling in yet another law-suit with Phillips over a technical dispute regarding South Pass 89 eliminated another cloud of uncertainty over the company's future revenue stream. And finally, the company was able to attract and retain a number of talented nonfamily oil and gas professionals who focused on drilling and exploration rather than internal family dynamics, power struggles, and racetracks.

Although I am unsure if anyone at Remington would agree, I hap-pen to believe there was a fourth factor involved: Tom's aggressive growth campaign, which probably gave the firm a strategic advantage it otherwise might not have had. Prior to Tom's tenure, Box Energy had been a passive, working-interest owner in a few prolific leases offshore. In the two and half years that he was CEO, Tom led the company into domestic areas the company had never ventured into before, such as South Texas, Arkansas, and Alabama.

During its lifespan of nine years, Remington was a huge bene-factor of a bullish energy market. From August of 1997 until it was sold to Cal-Dive in January of 2006, the price of crude rose as much as 242 percent while the price of natural gas increased approxi-mately 218 percent.

Though he went about it the wrong way, history proves one thing: Tom was right. We never should have sold Box Energy. At least he has the benefit of knowing he did everything in his power to keep this from happening. Those of us on the other side of the argument don't have such a luxury.

*D*on didn't just like working for Remington—he *loved* it. I think it was the only time in his life when he actually enjoyed his career. Too bad it came at such a high price. His ongoing relationship with Remington didn't sit well with the rest of us, particularly me. In an effort to cope with the guilt and tension, Don completely cut ties with all of us brothers, our wives, and our children. As a result, none of our children are close. They barely know each other.

Over the next five years, Don wouldn't speak to me. I tried reaching out to him during those years, including kids' birthdays, holidays, and other special occasions, but he never responded.

I have my doubts that he and I would have ever spoken again had it not been for his auto accident in 2002. A couple of days before Thanksgiving of that year, he went out with a buddy for a night on the town. He left a nightclub and drove himself home in his late-model Mercedes-Benz. He missed a turn, jumped a curb, and clipped a telephone pole.

The morning after his accident, the doctors couldn't tell us if he was going to make it or not. Thinking this might be the last time I'd ever see him, I sped over to the ICU unit at Parkland Hospital, where I found him strapped tightly to a bed. He was conscious and stable, but he couldn't utter a word. A series of tubes ran down his throat. The single-car accident left him with a spinal cord injury. For the next seven and a half years, he was a quadriplegic. The only thing he could control was his eyes.

For the first time in five years, I spoke to my oldest brother. I told him he'd been in a car wreck and was paralyzed but he was going to be all right. He nodded appreciatively. He was glad to see me; I could tell by his eyes. I knew he wanted me to stay, and so I did. I loved my brother, and it gave me a warm feeling to be around him again.

It was then, and only then, that he and I restored any kind of relationship. On the surface, we were cordial. Over the long term, however, the trauma done to our relationship, much like his injuries, was simply not reversible. Sad to say, Don and I were never able to fully reconcile our differences.

In January 2010, Don died of complications from his injury. His wife, Terri, asked me to speak at his memorial service. I talked about how much he influenced me, his love of music, his sense of humor, and how strong he was after his accident.

*A*fter my parents' divorce in 1986, Mom went on to marry an ex-air force pilot. Even though they were happily married for more than fourteen years, as Mother once told me, she never fell out of love with Cloyce. In 2007, she suffered a stroke and passed away at the age of eighty-one.

I spoke at her service as well. I talked about how pretty Fern was, but how her physical beauty paled in comparison to how beautiful she was on the inside. Her eulogy was one of the hardest things I've ever had to do. Still, I was deeply honored that my family allowed me do it.

*F*ive years after we sold the business, I went back to school to earn an MBA at one of the executive programs in Dallas. I wasn't sure what I wanted to do, but I knew my money wouldn't last forever. I needed a job, a new career. I thought an MBA might help.

I spent the next few years trying to rekindle my strained relationship with Don and finishing school, and I began to see things in a different light. With the added benefit of hindsight, I was able to see some of the mistakes that we'd made as a family, as well as many of the mistakes I'd made personally.

I held myself accountable for much of what went wrong. I had allowed too many people to influence me in a negative way. Deep down, I knew I could have saved our family's enterprise, but for reasons I've tried to explain in this book, I chose not to. Looking back, I realize that I lost sight of who I was. The fog of civil warfare did that to me, along with fear and greed. In the end, I let everyone down: my brothers, my cousins, my parents, my children, and most of all, myself.

I developed a deep need for absolution, to find some way to redeem myself for the turmoil caused by my family's collective failure. The more I yearned for such a thing, the more I had to accept that it would never happen for my family. I eventually decided that the only way to atone was to make a difference in the lives of other families who faced similar challenges.

In 2005 I formed Box Family Advisors, LLC, to motivate, educate, and support families in their quest toward family business continuity—and even more importantly, family harmony. Helping other families work through their own set of challenges has helped me achieve some measure of absolution. My practice is more than just a business; it is my calling. It's also a legacy: my father's, and my family's.

ACKNOWLEDGMENTS

David Lee Johnson was the first person to ever suggest that I write this book. David is a financial advisor with Morgan Stanley as well as a business analyst with CBS radio affiliate KRLD, in Dallas. We both went to Greenhill in the 1970s but didn't know each other during that time due to our age differences. In October of 1997, David and I ran into each other at our high school reunion, and it was then that he told me I needed to write this book.

That was almost twenty years ago.

Then, in 2010, a mutual friend introduced me to Jim "JW" Waggoner. JW was a financial advisor with a firm based in Sioux Falls, South Dakota. He and his business partners were planning to host a small gathering of their clients and wanted to find an interesting topic or speaker. After sharing some of my story with them over lunch, he invited me to travel to Sioux Falls and give my presentation. I was excited to do this, because they offered to pay me. This was my first speaking job.

A month or two later, I found myself in Sioux Falls. It was chilly up there, but the people couldn't have been warmer. My story seemed to resonate well with the audience that day. At the end, a well-dressed woman named Darlene Muth approached me and asked, "Where's your book?"

"I don't have one," I said.

"Well you better get one," she replied sharply.

From that point on, I began to think about how to write such a book. I knew it would be a difficult process, and yet, the more speaking I did, the louder and louder the voices became.

Finally, in April of 2012, I began the process in earnest. I thought it would take a year to finish. Instead, it took four.

First, I want to thank my own friends and family. I won't list their names here but they know who they are. I cannot overstate my appreciation for their help and support during the time that I was writing this book.

The second group of people I wish to thank are the friends that I made at the various Family Business Centers scattered across the country. These include Beth Adamson, John Butler, Rosalind Butler, Cindy Clarke, Ellie Frey, Chuck Gallagher, Ken Gilbert, Ed Hart, Kathleen Hoye, Peter Johnson, Lanie Jordan, Leslie McNabb, Jim Parker, John Schoen, and Bill Worthington.

Third, I'd like to thank the entire staff at Greenleaf Book Group, including Sam Alexander, Hobbs Allison, Bill Crawford, Steve Elizalde, Jen Glynn, Carrie Jones, Scott James, Pam Nordberg, Kris Pauls, Brian Phillips, Jeanne Thornton, and Nathan True.

Finally, I am thankful to the following people for their help and support in creating *Texas Patriarch*: Juli Baldwin, Mike Barr, Cindy Birne, Robert Birne, Bridget Boland, Kim Gatlin, Michael Gray, Susan Hamm, Janet Harris, Julie Hersh, Matthew Limpede, Bert Pigg, and Jenny Sommerfeld.

ABOUT THE AUTHOR

*D*ouglas D Box is an author, speaker, mediator, and family business consultant. Doug brings personal experience to his understanding of family dynamics, helping families with succession planning, corporate governance, dispute resolution, and family communication. Doug has also entertained audiences around the country at wealth-management conferences, trade associations, and family-business forums. He also serves as a guest lecturer at a number of universities on the topic of family business management.

In September of 2014, Doug published his first book, *Cutter Frisco: Growing Up on the Original Southfork Ranch*. Doug has been featured in a number of newspaper and magazine articles and has appeared on network television and radio.

The youngest of four sons, he grew up and worked in his family's oil and gas business. Doug received an MBA with honors from Baylor University, and a master of arts in dispute resolution from Southern Methodist University. He also holds a certificate in family business advising from the Family Firm Institute, in Boston. As an undergraduate, he obtained bachelor degrees in business administration and radio–TV–film from the University of Texas at Austin.

Doug lives in Dallas and has three children.